marie claire

comfort

Acknowledgments

A heartfelt thanks to Kay Scarlett and Juliet Rogers for allowing me, once again, to lose myself in the world of spoons, whisks and roasting tins.

A huge thank you to Marylouise Brammer for her time and unflagging enthusiasm, the result of which is a beautifully designed book. Fortunately we live at either ends of a long street and Hopscotch Café is somewhere in the middle. Many breakfasts and lunches were enjoyed there as the book grew from a single idea to a final mass of stunning images.

Jacqueline Blanchard rose to the challenge of organizing everything to do with this book including, or maybe especially, its author. A big thank you for your patience in calmly pulling all the threads together. For her support, knowledge and good cheer in the testing process a huge thank you to Heidi Flett. Thanks also to Michelle Lucia for her queries, patience and answers in the test kitchen. And for a cookbook to work, the words have to make sense, so a very big thanks to Zoë Harpham for keeping a sharp editorial eye on all my ramblings.

This is a book about real food and it would all be for nothing if the pages didn't make your mouth water. Once again Ross Dobson has been the patron saint of mixing bowls, cooking pots and market fresh ingredients. Thank you for all your hard work and for making all that is gorgeous seem so effortless. Mikkel Vang and Christine Rudolph again added the spice and magic of photography. A big hug to you both for the beautiful images that take us for a wander through farm gates, kitchen gardens, open fields and inviting kitchens.

Cookbooks not only take over the kitchen but also seem to seep into all areas of the home. As always the biggest thank you goes to Warwick, Ben and Sam for providing love, laughter and the important commodities of space and time. I'll apologize now for spending most Saturday mornings at the local growers' market and for filling the car with crunchy bread and strange vegetables!

marie claire

comfort

real simple food

michele cranston

photography by Mikkel Vang
styling by Christine Rudolph

whitecap

contents

real food

Great food doesn't have to be difficult or clever. It can be as simple as a perfectly ripe tomato or a salad of warm vegetables. When I first started working on this book, I held a single idyllic image in my mind. I thought about all the Saturdays that I've come home from the local growers' market with bundles of vine-ripened tomatoes, big bunches of aromatic herbs, heavy loads of assorted muddy potatoes and little brown bags filled with emerald green beans, feathery-topped fennel and earthy-toned mushrooms. I imagined a large table surrounded by friends and family, a pot on the stove, a roast in the oven and an idea for something sweetly seductive for dessert.

But thinking about my crowded local market made me wonder about modern food. We seem to have come to a point where there is a lot of talk about food, in all areas of the media, but I'm aware that there is a whole generation of people who haven't grown up with home-cooked meals. There's something interesting about the fact that we've reached the futuristic sounding 21st century and yet my local growers' market is crowded every weekend with city people wanting to buy food that has come directly from the farm. We seem to be indulging in a nostalgia for real food.

In this book I've resisted the temptation to be a food purist and demand that everything you buy be organic. However, I would hope that when possible you'll support the independent farmers who are out there growing beautiful produce. Treasure the food that you buy: go to the market and talk to the 'chicken man' and the woman whose passion it is to make cheese and churn butter. In other words, enjoy fresh, flavour-packed food, savour wonderful old-fashioned recipes for home-made produce, indulge in the occasionally extravagant ingredient and relish the wonderfully diverse range of foods that are now available to us.

Hopefully, the outcome of my pondering is a book about simple-to-cook, great-tasting food that will bring wholesome, real ingredients to life and make your mouth water in anticipation.

spoon

tasting and stirring, dolloping anc

serving, scooping and swirling

34

Stirring and dolloping...

Nothing is more integral to the process of cooking than the humble spoon. Spoons worn down by a lifetime of smooth turns through custards, sauces and meaty stews. Wooden spoons with the odd burn and scar from reckless use. Spoons that help add a hint of intense flavour, such as a swirl of oil or a dollop of rich cream.

apricot and rhubarb with ginger spiced yoghurt

4 cm (1 1/2 inch) piece of fresh ginger
3 cardamom pods, split
1/2 teaspoon honey
4 tablespoons caster (superfine) sugar
400 g (14 oz/1 bunch) rhubarb
4 apricots
250 g (9 oz/1 cup) plain yoghurt

Preheat the oven to 200°C (400°F/Gas 6). Line a baking tray with baking paper. Peel the ginger and slice it into four rounds. Pour 150 ml (5 fl oz) of water into a saucepan and add the ginger, cardamom pods, honey and 2 tablespoons of the sugar. Heat over medium heat until the liquid begins to thicken and forms a syrup, then remove the pan from the heat and set aside.

Trim the rhubarb and cut it into 8 cm (3 1/4 inch) lengths. Rinse under cold running water, then put the pieces of rhubarb into a bowl. Add the remaining sugar to the bowl and toss so that the rhubarb is well coated. Put the rhubarb on the baking tray, reserving the sugary juices in the bowl.

Cut the apricots in half, remove the stones and add the halves to the rhubarb. Swirl a tablespoon of water into the sugar that remains in the bowl and drizzle it over the apricots. Cover the fruit with another sheet of baking paper, then top with a larger sheet of foil to hold it in place. Bake for 15 minutes, or until the rhubarb is soft. Remove and allow to cool. Strain the syrup over the yoghurt and lightly fold together before serving with the baked fruit. Serves 4

pancakes with chocolate butter

150 g (5 1/2 oz) unsalted butter, softened
50 g (1 3/4 oz) dark eating chocolate
1/4 teaspoon ground cinnamon
4 tablespoons maple syrup
90 g (3 1/4 oz/3/4 cup) plain (all-purpose) flour
1 heaped teaspoon baking powder
1 tablespoon caster (superfine) sugar
1 egg, lightly beaten
250 ml (9 fl oz/1 cup) milk
1 teaspoon natural vanilla extract
unsalted butter, extra, for cooking
maple syrup, extra, to serve
bottled morello cherries, drained, or fresh raspberries, to serve (optional)

To make the chocolate butter, put the butter, chocolate, cinnamon and maple syrup in a food processor and blend to form a smooth butter. Spoon onto a length of plastic wrap and roll up to form a log. Store in the refrigerator until ready to serve.

To make the pancake batter, sift the flour into a bowl and add the baking powder, caster sugar and a pinch of salt, then make a well in the centre. In a separate bowl, whisk together the egg, milk and vanilla extract. Pour the milk mixture into the dry ingredients and whisk until the batter is smooth. Cover and allow to chill in the refrigerator for 30 minutes.

Remove the chocolate butter and the batter from the refrigerator. Grease a small non-stick frying pan with the extra butter and place over medium heat. As the butter begins to sizzle, spoon the batter into the pan to form two to three 8 cm (3 1/4 inch) rounds.

Cook the pancakes for a minute, or until the top surface begins to bubble. Flip over and cook for a further minute. Repeat with the remaining batter, stacking the cooked pancakes on a plate as you go. Divide among four serving plates and top with slices of the chocolate butter and an extra drizzle of maple syrup. Serve as is or with morello cherries or fresh raspberries. Serves 4

a luscious mix of spiced yoghurt and soft-baked fruit

Opposite: apricot and rhubarb with ginger spiced yoghurt
Over: pancakes with chocolate butter

dill pancakes with smoked salmon

200 g (7 oz/heaped 1 2/3 cups) plain (all-purpose) flour
1/2 teaspoon salt
2 teaspoons baking powder
2 eggs
250 ml (9 fl oz/1 cup) milk
grated zest of 1 lemon
1 tablespoon finely chopped dill
1 tablespoon butter
1 tablespoon lemon juice
100 g (3 1/2 oz/heaped 1/3 cup) crème fraîche
12 slices of smoked salmon, cut in half
dill sprigs, to serve

To make the batter, sift the flour and salt into a bowl. Stir in the baking powder, then make a well in the centre. In a separate bowl, beat the eggs and milk together. Pour the milk mixture into the well in the dry ingredients and whisk together thoroughly. Stir in the grated lemon zest and chopped dill. Allow the batter to rest at room temperature for 10 minutes.

Heat a non-stick frying pan over medium heat and grease the surface with a little of the butter. Using 1 tablespoon at a time, drop spoonfuls of batter onto the hot surface and cook until the top surface of the pancake begins to bubble. Flip over and cook for a further minute, then remove to a plate, stacking the pancakes to keep warm. Repeat with the remaining batter — you should make around 24.

Fold the lemon juice through the crème fraîche and season with a little freshly ground black pepper.

Top the pancakes with smoked salmon, a spoonful of the lemony crème fraîche and a sprig of dill. Makes 24

corn fritters

125 g (4 1/2 oz/1 cup) plain (all-purpose) flour
1 teaspoon baking powder
1 teaspoon smoked paprika
1 tablespoon sugar
1 teaspoon sea salt
2 eggs
125 ml (4 fl oz/1/2 cup) milk
4 corn cobs
1/2 red capsicum (pepper), diced
4 spring onions (scallions), finely sliced
90 g (3 1/4 oz/1 bunch) coriander (cilantro), chopped
4 tablespoons vegetable oil
crisp bacon or fried eggs, to serve

Sift the flour, baking powder and paprika into a large bowl, stir in the sugar and salt and make a well in the centre. In a separate bowl, whisk together the eggs and milk. Gradually add the liquid ingredients to the dry, stirring to ensure that you have a stiff, lump-free batter. Cover and refrigerate until ready to use.

With a sharp knife, cut the corn kernels away from the cobs and put the kernels in a large bowl. Add the capsicum, spring onion and coriander. Toss to combine.

Just before serving, slowly work the batter into the fresh ingredients. Heat 2 tablespoons of the oil in a large non-stick frying pan over medium heat. Using 1 tablespoon at a time, drop spoonfuls of batter onto the hot surface. Cook for a few minutes, or until the underside is golden, then flip and cook for a further 2 minutes until quite crisp. Remove from the pan and keep warm while you make the rest of the fritters, adding more oil when necessary — you should make around 30. Serve with bacon or fried eggs. Serves 6

crab omelettes

3 eggs
1 tablespoon mirin
1/2 teaspoon soy sauce
250 g (9 oz/1 1/4 cups) fresh crabmeat, shredded
1 teaspoon lemon juice
1 teaspoon olive oil
90 g (3 1/4 oz/1 cup) bean sprouts
1 large handful coriander (cilantro) leaves
2 teaspoons vegetable oil
2 spring onions (scallions), sliced on the diagonal
1 large red chilli, seeded and very finely sliced

Whisk together the eggs, mirin and soy sauce in a small bowl. Season with pepper and sea salt.

In a separate bowl, combine the crabmeat, lemon juice and olive oil. Add the sprouts and coriander, season, then toss to combine.

Heat a small non-stick frying pan over medium heat and add 1/2 teaspoon of the vegetable oil. Ladle in one-quarter of the egg mixture and swirl it around so that the egg thinly coats the base of the pan. Continue to cook until the egg has cooked through, then remove by sliding the omelette out onto a warmed plate. Repeat with the remaining mixture, adding oil to the pan as it is needed, until you have four thin omelettes.

Place each of the omelettes on a warmed serving plate, add one-quarter of the crab mixture and fold half the omelette over the filling. Sprinkle with the spring onion and chilli, then serve immediately. Serves 4

Opposite: dill pancakes with smoked salmon
Over: corn fritters; crab omelettes

chicken and leek soup

1 small whole organic chicken (about 1 kg/2 lb 4 oz)
a few flat-leaf (Italian) parsley sprigs
2 carrots, peeled and roughly chopped
1 small handful pearl barley or white rice
2 teaspoons sea salt
2 tablespoons butter
2 large leeks, rinsed and finely sliced
4 large all-purpose potatoes, peeled and diced
1 handful flat-leaf (Italian) parsley, roughly chopped

Rinse the chicken under running water, inside and out. Remove any chunks of fat from the cavity, then place the chicken into a large saucepan along with the parsley sprigs, carrot and barley or rice. Fill the pan with water and bring to the boil. Skim away any foam that rises to the surface. Add the salt and reduce the heat to low. Allow to simmer gently for 2 hours, or until the meat is falling from the bones of the chicken.

Remove the chicken from the stock, then strain the stock through a colander which is positioned over a large bowl. Skim any fat from the surface of the stock. Clean the saucepan and return it to the stove. Add the butter and sauté the leek until soft. Pour in the strained chicken stock, add the potato and continue to cook over medium heat for 8–10 minutes, or until the potato is tender when pierced with a skewer.

Meanwhile, remove and roughly chop the chicken flesh, discarding any skin. A few minutes before you are ready to serve, return the chicken meat to the soup along with the roughly chopped parsley. Season to taste with sea salt. Serves 4

smoked trout salad

1 red onion
1 tablespoon sea salt
1 teaspoon sugar
3 tablespoons lemon juice
1 egg yolk
4 tablespoons olive oil
1 telegraph (long) cucumber
1 teaspoon poppy seeds
2 x 200 g (7 oz) smoked river trout
2 large handfuls picked watercress sprigs

Peel the onion, then cut it in half. Finely slice the onion halves into thin half moons. Put the onion into a bowl and add the salt. Toss several times to ensure that the onion is well coated, then set aside for 30 minutes.

Drain the liquid from the onion, then rinse under cold running water before squeezing out any excess liquid. Return the onion to a clean bowl and add the sugar and 2 tablespoons of the lemon juice. Stir to combine, then set to one side for a further 30 minutes.

Put the egg yolk in a small bowl with the remaining lemon juice. Whisk until creamy, then slowly pour in the olive oil, whisking all the time until it forms a thin mayonnaise. Season to taste with sea salt and freshly ground black pepper.

Peel the cucumber and slice it in half lengthways. Using a teaspoon, remove the seeds from the centre of the cucumber, then finely slice the flesh. Put the cucumber pieces into a bowl and toss with the poppy seeds. Remove the skin from the trout, then gently pull away the flesh, ensuring that you remove all bones.

Arrange the watercress sprigs on four serving plates. Top with the cucumber and then the trout pieces. Drizzle with the lemon dressing and place a pile of the pink onions in the centre. Serves 4

a bowl full of feel-good chicken soup

Opposite: chicken and leek soup
Over: smoked trout salad

mushroom ragout on brioche

10 g (1/4 oz) dried porcini mushrooms
2 tablespoons olive oil
1 onion (preferably brown), diced
2 garlic cloves, finely chopped
2 slices of bacon, finely chopped
500 g (1 lb 2 oz) mixed mushrooms, such as Swiss brown, shiitake, morels and field, stems removed
250 ml (9 fl oz/1 cup) red wine
2 tablespoons tomato paste (concentrated purée)
4 thick slices of brioche
1 tablespoon cornflour (cornstarch)
2 handfuls flat-leaf (Italian) parsley, roughly chopped
50 g (13/4 oz/1/2 cup) shaved pecorino cheese

Put the dried porcini mushrooms in a small bowl and cover with 250 ml (9 fl oz/1 cup) of boiling water. Allow to soak for 15 minutes.

Heat the oil in a saucepan over medium heat, add the onion, garlic and bacon and cook for 5 minutes, or until the onion is soft and transparent. Thickly slice all the fresh mushrooms and add them to the saucepan. Strain the soaking mushrooms over the pan so that the soaking liquid drains into the pan. Finely chop the soaked mushrooms and add them to the pan along with the wine, tomato paste and a little salt and pepper. Cover with a lid and simmer for 40 minutes, or until the mushrooms have cooked and all the flavours are well combined.

Toast the brioche. Meanwhile, put the cornflour in a small bowl with 3 tablespoons of water and stir until the cornflour has dissolved. Add the cornflour paste to the mushrooms and stir until the mixture has thickened, then remove the pan from the heat. Sprinkle with the chopped parsley.

Place the toasted brioche onto four serving plates and top with the mushroom ragout. Top with the shaved pecorino, then serve. Serves 4

spiced carrot soup

21/2 tablespoons butter
1 red onion, diced
1 teaspoon ground cumin
3 tablespoons red lentils
500 g (1 lb 2 oz) carrots, peeled and finely chopped
1.5 litres (52 fl oz/6 cups) vegetable stock (Basics)
ground cumin, extra, or thick (double/heavy) cream, to serve

Melt the butter in a saucepan over medium heat, then add the onion and cumin. Cook until the onion is soft and transparent, then add the lentils and carrot. Stir for a minute before pouring in the stock. Bring to the boil, then reduce the heat to a slow simmer. Continue to cook for 40 minutes, or until the carrot is soft and beginning to fall apart.

Remove the pan from the heat and allow to cool slightly. Transfer the mixture to a blender, a few ladlefuls at a time, and blend to a smooth purée. Return to a clean saucepan and heat over low heat when ready to serve. Season with sea salt and freshly ground black pepper. Serve with a sprinkle of ground cumin or a dollop of cream. Serves 4 as a starter

buttery brioche and the earthy flavour of mushrooms

Opposite: mushroom ragout on brioche
Over: spiced carrot soup

roast pumpkin and coconut soup

1 kg (2 lb 4 oz) jap or kent pumpkin, peeled and cut into chunks
2 tablespoons olive oil
1 garlic clove, finely sliced
2 leeks, rinsed and finely sliced
1 red chilli, seeded and finely chopped
500 ml (17 fl oz/2 cups) vegetable stock (Basics)
200 ml (7 fl oz) coconut milk
1 handful coriander (cilantro) leaves

Preheat the oven to 180°C (350°F/Gas 4). Put the pumpkin in a roasting tin and roast for 30 minutes, or until cooked through and golden brown.

Put the oil in a large saucepan with the garlic and leek. Cook over medium heat until the leek is soft and transparent. Add the pumpkin, chilli and stock and simmer for 10 minutes. Remove from the heat and allow to cool slightly.

Transfer the soup mixture to a blender and blend until smooth. Return to a clean saucepan and stir in the coconut milk. Reheat over medium heat, then ladle into four bowls and scatter with coriander. Serves 4

blue-eye with fennel and tomato broth

1 small fennel bulb
1 tablespoon butter
1 small leek, rinsed and finely sliced
3 ripe tomatoes, finely chopped
1 litre (35 fl oz/4 cups) fish stock (Basics)
2 tablespoons lemon juice
4 x 100 g ($3\frac{1}{2}$ oz) blue-eye cod fillets
4 tablespoons aïoli (Basics)
10 basil leaves, roughly torn

Trim the fennel bulb, reserving the feathery tops, then cut the bulb in half and finely slice it.

Melt the butter in a large saucepan over medium heat, add the leek and cook until soft, then add the tomato, sliced fennel and stock. Bring to the boil, then reduce the heat, cover and simmer for 15 minutes. Add the lemon juice and fish and cover. Cook for 7 minutes, or until the fish is opaque and cooked through.

Lift out the fish and divide among four warmed pasta bowls. Ladle over the broth and top with a spoonful of aïoli. Garnish with the fennel tops and basil. Serves 4

lemon risotto with seared prawns

1 litre (35 fl oz/4 cups) fish or vegetable stock (Basics)
2 tablespoons butter
2 garlic cloves, finely chopped
2 leeks, rinsed and finely sliced
finely grated zest and juice of 1 lemon
325 g ($11\frac{1}{2}$ oz/$1\frac{1}{2}$ cups) risotto rice
4 tablespoons grated parmesan cheese
16 raw king prawns (shrimp), peeled and deveined, tails intact
extra virgin olive oil, to serve
flat-leaf (Italian) parsley, to serve

Bring the stock to the boil in a saucepan, then reduce to a low simmer.

Melt the butter in a large saucepan over medium heat. Add the garlic and leek and sauté until the leek is soft and transparent. Add the grated lemon zest and rice and stir for 1 minute until the rice is well coated and the grains are glossy.

Add 250 ml (9 fl oz/1 cup) of stock to the rice and simmer, stirring until it is completely absorbed. Repeat twice more, allowing the stock to absorb before adding the next batch. Cook until all the liquid has been absorbed, then test the rice to see if it is *al dente*. If it needs more cooking, pour in the remaining stock and stir until absorbed. Add half the lemon juice and the freshly grated parmesan and lightly fold it through the risotto. Remove the pan from the heat while you cook the prawns.

Quickly heat a large frying pan over high heat and sear the prawns on both sides for a few minutes, or until the flesh is pink and opaque. Pour the remaining lemon juice over the prawns, then remove from the heat. Spoon the risotto into four warmed pasta bowls and top with the prawns. Serve with a drizzle of extra virgin olive oil and a scattering of parsley. Serves 4

Opposite: roast pumpkin and coconut soup
Over: blue-eye with fennel and tomato broth; lemon risotto with seared prawns

chicken and vermouth risotto

750 ml (26 fl oz/3 cups) chicken stock (Basics)
2 tablespoons butter
2 boneless, skinless chicken breasts, finely sliced
2 garlic cloves, finely chopped
2 onions, finely sliced
1 tablespoon thyme leaves
325 g (11 1/2 oz/1 1/2 cups) risotto rice
250 ml (9 fl oz/1 cup) dry vermouth
50 g (1 3/4 oz/1/2 cup) finely grated parmesan cheese
1 handful flat-leaf (Italian) parsley, roughly chopped

Bring the stock to the boil in a saucepan, then reduce to a low simmer.

Preheat the oven to 130°C (250°F/Gas 1). Melt the butter in a large saucepan over medium heat. Add the chicken slices and cook until lightly golden on both sides. Remove the chicken slices to an ovenproof plate, cover tightly with foil and keep in the oven until ready to serve.

Add the garlic, onion and thyme to the pan. Cook until the onion is soft and transparent, then add the rice. Stir for a minute until the rice is well coated and the grains are glossy. Pour in the vermouth and simmer, stirring until it is completely absorbed.

Add 250 ml (9 fl oz/1 cup) of stock to the rice and simmer, stirring until it is completely absorbed. Ladle in another 250 ml (9 fl oz/1 cup) of stock and add half the parmesan. Cook, stirring constantly, until all the liquid has been absorbed, then test the rice to see if it is *al dente*. If it needs more cooking, add a little more stock and cook until absorbed. Spoon the risotto into four warmed pasta bowls and top with the chicken, parsley and remaining parmesan. Serves 4

tomato and prosciutto risotto

1 litre (35 fl oz/4 cups) chicken or vegetable stock (Basics)
4 large slices of prosciutto, cut in half crossways
2 tablespoons butter
2 garlic cloves, finely chopped
2 leeks, rinsed and finely sliced
325 g (11 1/2 oz/1 1/2 cups) risotto rice
3 ripe roma (plum) tomatoes, diced
2 tablespoons dry sherry
4 tablespoons grated parmesan cheese
extra virgin olive oil, to serve
rocket (arugula) or fresh basil, to serve

Bring the stock to the boil in a saucepan, then reduce to a low simmer.

Heat a large saucepan over medium heat and add the prosciutto. Cook on both sides until golden and crisp. Remove and drain on paper towels. Add the butter, garlic and leek to the saucepan and sauté for 4–5 minutes, or until the leek is soft and transparent. Add the rice and stir for a minute until the rice is well coated and the grains are glossy.

Ladle 250 ml (9 fl oz/1 cup) of stock into the pan and simmer, stirring until it is completely absorbed. Add another 250 ml (9 fl oz/1 cup) of stock and the diced tomato. Cook, stirring, for a further few minutes until the stock is completely absorbed, then add another 250 ml (9 fl oz/1 cup) of stock. Cook until all the liquid has been absorbed, then test the rice to see if it is *al dente*. If it needs more cooking, add the remaining stock. Splash in the sherry and add half the parmesan, then lightly fold through the risotto. Spoon into four warmed pasta bowls and sprinkle with the remaining parmesan. Crumble the prosciutto into smaller pieces and scatter over the risotto. Drizzle with a little extra virgin olive oil and serve with a rocket salad. Serves 4

warming comfort food by the spoonful

Opposite: chicken and vermouth risotto
Over: tomato and prosciutto risotto

herby harissa

Remove the seeds, membrane and skin of 1 roasted red capsicum (Basics). Roughly chop the flesh and put it in a food processor with 2 roughly chopped garlic cloves, 4 seeded and roughly chopped red chillies, 1 teaspoon ground coriander, 1 teaspoon ground cumin, 90 g (3 1/4 oz/1 bunch) coriander (cilantro), roughly chopped, 3 tablespoons olive oil and 1 tablespoon lemon juice. Process to form a thick sauce. Serve with roast chicken, chargrilled tuna and fried eggs. This will keep in an airtight container in the refrigerator for several weeks. Makes about 300 g (10 1/2 oz/1 cup)

preserved lemon and mint sauce

Put 2 large handfuls flat-leaf (Italian) parsley, 30 mint leaves, 1 tablespoon finely chopped preserved lemon, 3 teaspoons lemon juice and 125 ml (4 fl oz/1/2 cup) olive oil in a food processor or blender and blend until smooth. Serve with roast chicken, chargrilled blue-eye cod or baked salmon. This will keep in an airtight container in the refrigerator for several weeks. Makes about 250 ml (9 fl oz/1 cup)

roast tomato sauce

Preheat the oven to 180°C (350°F/Gas 4). Cut 500 g (1 lb 2 oz) roma (plum) tomatoes into quarters, then put on a baking tray. Sprinkle with 1 teaspoon each of sugar and salt. Roast for 40 minutes, or until the tomatoes are beginning to blacken at the edges. Put the tomatoes in a food processor or blender with 1 tablespoon pomegranate molasses, 10 basil leaves, 1 roughly chopped garlic clove and 1 teaspoon ground cumin and blend to form a smooth sauce. Season well with sea salt and freshly ground black pepper. Serve with chargrilled lamb, beef or seared fresh tuna. This will keep in an airtight container in the refrigerator for several weeks. Makes about 250 ml (9 fl oz/1 cup)

tapenade

Put 80 g (2¾ oz/½ cup) pitted kalamata olives, 1 roughly chopped garlic clove, 1 handful flat-leaf (Italian) parsley, roughly chopped, 10 basil leaves, 2 anchovy fillets, 1 teaspoon salted capers, rinsed and drained, and 3 tablespoons extra virgin olive oil in a blender or food processor and blend to a rough paste. Season with freshly ground black pepper to taste. Serve with seared lamb or beef. This will keep in an airtight container in the refrigerator for several weeks. Makes about 300 g (10½ oz/1 cup)

fig and goat's cheese salad

1 teaspoon wild flower honey
1 teaspoon balsamic vinegar
1 teaspoon wholegrain mustard
3 teaspoons extra virgin olive oil
6 slices of prosciutto
6 large figs
100 g (3 1/2 oz/3 cups) wild rocket (arugula) leaves
100 g (3 1/2 oz) goat's cheese, cut into 4 slices

Combine the honey, vinegar, mustard and olive oil in a large bowl and stir to combine.

Heat a non-stick frying pan over medium heat and fry the prosciutto until crisp and golden. Remove from the pan and drain on paper towels.

Finely slice the figs and arrange the slices over four plates. Stir the dressing one more time, then add the rocket to the dressing and toss lightly. Crumble the prosciutto over the rocket and toss again before piling the salad onto the sliced figs. Top each of the salads with a slice of goat's cheese. Serves 4

minestrone

150 g (5 1/2 oz/3/4 cup) dried cannellini (white) beans
2 tablespoons butter
100 g (3 1/2 oz) pancetta, finely chopped
2 red onions, finely chopped
2 carrots, peeled and grated
2 celery stalks, finely sliced
3 large ripe tomatoes, roughly chopped
1 litre (35 fl oz/4 cups) chicken or vegetable stock (Basics)
1 bay leaf
1 rosemary sprig
2 zucchini (courgettes), diced
100 g (3 1/2 oz) green beans, trimmed and cut into 2 cm (3/4 inch) lengths
60 g (2 1/4 oz/1/3 cup) risoni
2 tablespoons tomato paste (concentrated purée)
pesto (Basics), to serve (optional)

Soak the dried beans overnight in plenty of water. Drain the beans.

Heat the butter in a large saucepan over medium heat. Add the pancetta and beans and cook for a minute before adding the onion, carrot and celery. Cook until the onion is soft and transparent, then add the tomato, stock, bay leaf, rosemary and 500 ml (17 fl oz/2 cups) of water. Bring to the boil, then reduce the heat to a gentle simmer and cook for 40 minutes, or until the beans are cooked through.

Add the zucchini, green beans, risoni and tomato paste and cook for a further 30 minutes, stirring often, until the risoni is *al dente*. Remove the bay leaf and rosemary sprig. Season to taste with sea salt and freshly ground black pepper. Serve as is or with a spoonful of pesto. Serves 4–6

tangy honey, ripe figs and creamy goat's cheese

Opposite: fig and goat's cheese salad
Over: minestrone

ginger parfait with a mulled wine syrup

1 vanilla bean
125 g (4 1/2 oz/heaped 1/2 cup) caster (superfine) sugar
4 cm (1 1/2 inch) piece of fresh ginger, peeled and roughly cut
5 egg yolks
500 g (1 lb 2 oz/2 cups) crème fraîche or sour cream
250 ml (9 fl oz/1 cup) red wine
110 g (3 3/4 oz/1/2 cup) sugar
1 cinnamon stick
2 cloves
2 cardamom pods, crushed

To make the ginger parfait, rub the vanilla bean between your fingertips to soften it, then split it along its length and use the tip of a knife to scrape out the seeds into a small heavy-based saucepan. Add the vanilla bean, caster sugar, ginger and 125 ml (4 fl oz/1/2 cup) of water. Place the pan over medium heat and allow to simmer for 5 minutes, or until you have a syrup. Strain the syrup into a bowl.

Whisk the egg yolks in a large bowl until light and fluffy, then add the warm sugar syrup. Whisk for a minute, then add the crème fraîche and whisk again to combine. Pour into an 8 x 22 cm (3 1/4 x 8 1/2 inch) loaf (bar) tin lined with baking paper. Freeze overnight.

To make the mulled wine syrup, pour the wine into a small saucepan and add the white sugar and spices. Bring to the boil, then reduce the heat and simmer for 10 minutes before straining into a bowl. Allow the syrup to cool completely.

Cut the ginger parfait into thick slices. Place the slices onto a chilled plate and drizzle with the mulled wine syrup. Serves 6

ginger parfait with a mulled wine syrup

creamed rice with pomegranate molasses

1 tablespoon pomegranate molasses
2 tablespoons soft brown sugar
110 g (3 3/4 oz/1/2 cup) short-grain white rice
1 vanilla bean
500 ml (17 fl oz/2 cups) milk
4 tablespoons caster (superfine) sugar
125 ml (4 fl oz/1/2 cup) pouring (whipping) cream, whipped
fresh pomegranate seeds, mango slices or strawberries, to serve

Put the molasses, brown sugar and 1 tablespoon of boiling water in a small bowl and stir until the sugar has dissolved. Set aside.

Rinse the rice in cold water, then drain. Rub the vanilla bean between your fingertips to soften it, then split it along its length. Using the tip of a knife, scrape most of the seeds into a saucepan. Add the vanilla bean, milk and sugar to the pan and bring it almost to the boil. Add the rice and reduce the heat to low and simmer gently for 30 minutes, stirring occasionally.

When the rice has cooked, remove the pan from the heat and lift out the vanilla bean. Transfer the rice to a bowl and allow to cool completely.

When the mixture has cooled, fold through the whipped cream. Divide the creamed rice among six bowls, then drizzle with some of the pomegranate molasses syrup and serve with fresh pomegranate seeds, mango slices or strawberries. Serves 6

apple 'cake' with vanilla syrup

165 g (5 3/4 oz/3/4 cup) sugar
185 ml (6 fl oz/3/4 cup) apple juice
juice of 1 lemon
1 vanilla bean
10 green apples
thick (double/heavy) cream or vanilla ice cream (Basics), to serve

Preheat the oven to 120°C (235°F/Gas 1/2). Grease and line a 20 cm (8 inch) spring-form cake tin with baking paper. Sit the tin on a large sheet of foil and fold the foil up around the side of the tin — this should ensure that the syrup doesn't escape. Place the spring-form tin into a roasting tin.

Put the sugar, apple and lemon juice in a saucepan. Rub the vanilla bean between your fingertips to soften it, then split it along its length and use the tip of a knife to scrape out the seeds into the juice. Add the bean to the saucepan and bring to the boil, stirring until the sugar has dissolved. Reduce the heat to low and simmer for 10 minutes.

Peel the apples, then use an apple corer to remove the core from the apples, leaving the fruit in one piece. Finely slice the apples crossways to form thin circles. Layer the slices in the cake tin, lightly brushing each layer with some of the vanilla syrup. Place the roasting tin into the oven and bake for 4 hours. The 'cake' will be lightly golden on top and will have shrunk quite considerably. Allow to cool, then turn out onto a plate and serve in thick wedges with cream or ice cream. Serves 6–8

an old favourite meets the tang of pomegranate

Opposite: creamed rice with pomegranate molasses
Over: apple 'cake' with vanilla syrup

THE

vanilla ice cream with drunken chocolate sauce

150 ml (5 fl oz) pouring (whipping) cream
1 tablespoon soft brown sugar
1 1/2 tablespoons butter
50 g (1 3/4 oz) dark eating chocolate, broken into pieces
2 tablespoons liqueur, such as Tia Maria or Frangelico
1 litre (35 fl oz/4 cups) vanilla ice cream (Basics)
almond biscotti (Basics) or small wafers, to serve

Put the cream, sugar and butter in a small saucepan over low heat. When the butter has melted, add the chocolate and stir lightly until it has melted and is well combined with the cream. Remove from the heat and add the liqueur. Stir and allow to cool slightly.

Spoon the ice cream into four bowls and spoon over the warm chocolate sauce. Serve with almond biscotti or small wafers. Serves 4–6

custard with nectarines and blueberries

custard
250 ml (9 fl oz/1 cup) milk
250 ml (9 fl oz/1 cup) pouring (whipping) cream
1 vanilla bean
4 egg yolks
4 tablespoons caster (superfine) sugar

2 tablespoons caster (superfine) sugar
4 nectarines, sliced
150 g (5 1/2 oz/1 cup) blueberries

To make the custard, pour the milk and cream into a heavy-based saucepan. Lightly rub the vanilla bean between your fingertips to soften it. Using the tip of a small sharp knife, split the bean in half along its length and add it to the milk. Put the saucepan over medium heat and bring the mixture just to simmering point, then remove the pan from the heat.

Whisk the egg yolks with the sugar in a large bowl until the mixture is light and creamy. Whisk a little of the warm milk mixture into the eggs before adding the remaining liquid. Remove the vanilla bean and set aside, then whisk to combine.

Rinse and dry the saucepan, then return the mixture to the clean saucepan. Scrape the inside of the vanilla bean to remove the last of the seeds, then add these to the liquid. Cook over medium heat, stirring constantly with a wooden spoon, until the mixture thickens and coats the back of the spoon. If a line remains after you have dragged your finger across the spoon, then the custard is ready. Quickly remove to a chilled bowl and continue to whisk until it has slightly cooled. If serving cold, allow to cool completely before covering and chilling in the refrigerator.

Just before serving, prepare the fruit. Put the sugar in a deep frying pan with 1 tablespoon of water. Heat over low heat, swirling the mixture a little so that the sugar dissolves. Add the nectarine slices, swirl once, then cover with a lid. Cook over low heat for 4 minutes. Remove the lid and add the blueberries. Swirl a few more times until all the blueberries are glossy. Remove from the heat and divide among four bowls. Serve with the custard. Serves 4

Opposite: vanilla ice cream with drunken chocolate sauce
Over: custard with nectarines and blueberries

hazelnut affogato

375 ml (13 fl oz/1 1/2 cups) milk
250 ml (9 fl oz/1 cup) pouring (whipping) cream
2 tablespoons roast hazelnuts, finely ground
4 egg yolks
125 g (4 1/2 oz/heaped 1/2 cup) caster (superfine) sugar
4 teaspoons hazelnut or coffee liqueur
4 espresso cups of coffee

To make the ice cream, pour the milk and cream into a heavy-based saucepan and add the ground hazelnuts. Put the saucepan over medium heat and bring the mixture just to simmering point. Remove from the heat.

Whisk the egg yolks with the caster sugar in a large bowl until light and creamy. Whisk in a little of the warm milk mixture before adding the remaining liquid, then whisk to combine.

Rinse and dry the saucepan, then return the mixture to the clean saucepan. Cook over medium heat, stirring constantly with a wooden spoon, until the mixture thickens and coats the back of the spoon. Remove from the heat and strain into a chilled bowl. Allow to cool completely before churning in an ice-cream machine according to the manufacturer's instructions. Spoon into a container and freeze for at least 1 hour until ready to serve.

To serve, place 2 small scoops of ice cream into a small heatproof glass or cup, pour a teaspoon of liqueur over each and serve with an espresso or small cup of strong coffee. To eat, simply pour the coffee over the ice cream and enjoy. Serves 4 (makes enough ice cream for 10 serves)

hazelnut affogato

eton mess

Remove the hulls from 500 g (1 lb 2 oz/3 1/3 cups) strawberries, then cut them in half and put in a large bowl. Sprinkle with 1 tablespoon caster (superfine) sugar and lightly toss so all the fruit is coated. Set aside for 10 minutes. Smash 4 meringues (Basics) into several pieces. Whip 300 ml (10 1/2 fl oz) pouring (whipping) cream in a separate bowl and fold in 1 teaspoon natural vanilla extract. Layer the strawberries, broken meringue and whipped cream into four bowls and serve immediately. Serves 4

panettone trifle

Lightly toast 100 g (3 1/2 oz/heaped 1 cup) flaked almonds under the grill (broiler) or in a dry frying pan, then set aside. Separate the whites and yolks of 2 eggs. Whisk the egg whites in a clean bowl until soft peaks form. Put the egg yolks, 250 g (9 oz/heaped 1 cup) mascarpone, 3 tablespoons Tia Maria and 3 tablespoons caster (superfine) sugar in a separate bowl and stir to combine. Lightly fold the egg whites into the mascarpone mixture until all the ingredients are well combined. Pour 4 tablespoons strong coffee and 2 tablespoons marsala into a bowl. Tear 200 g (7 oz) panettone into bite-sized pieces and dip the pieces into the coffee. Layer the mascarpone cream with the almonds and dipped panettone pieces, finishing with the mascarpone cream and a final sprinkle of almonds. Serves 4

sweet mascarpone

Separate the whites and yolks of 2 eggs. Whisk the egg whites in a clean bowl until soft peaks form. Put the yolks, 250 g (9 oz/heaped 1 cup) mascarpone, 2–3 tablespoons caster (superfine) sugar, 1 teaspoon finely grated orange zest and 2 tablespoons Grand Marnier in a separate bowl and stir to combine. Lightly fold the egg whites into the mascarpone mixture until all the ingredients are well combined. Serve with fresh figs, grilled (broiled) peaches or poached pears. Serves 4

drunken chocolate mousse

Put 150 g (5 1/2 oz) chopped dark eating chocolate and 4 tablespoons strong coffee in a small bowl over a simmering saucepan of water, without letting the bowl touch the water. When the chocolate has melted, stir together, then remove the pan from the heat. Break 3 eggs and separate the whites and yolks. Whisk the egg yolks with 1 teaspoon natural vanilla extract, then stir in the melted chocolate. When the mixture is smooth, stir in 3–4 tablespoons brandy. Whisk the egg whites in a separate bowl until quite firm peaks form, then add 3 tablespoons soft brown sugar and continue to whisk until stiff peaks form. Fold in the chocolate mixture and 100 ml (3 1/2 fl oz) whipped cream. Cover and chill in the refrigerator for at least 1 hour or until ready to serve. Serves 4

table

plates and platters, knives

and forks, cups and bowls

Food to share...

A stack of plates, glasses polished to a reflective gleam, the snap of crisp linen and the collision of friends and family at the table. Food is all about gathering, sharing, tasting, indulging and enjoying. All of which can happen around a Sunday roast or a simple bowl of olives.

marinated olives

Finely slice 1 lemon and put the slices in a large bowl with 500 g (1 lb 2 oz) mixed unpitted olives, 2 crushed garlic cloves, 1 seeded and sliced red chilli, several lemon thyme sprigs, 1 rosemary sprig and 4 tablespoons extra virgin olive oil and toss to combine. Cover and allow to marinate in the refrigerator overnight. If you plan to eat these at a later date, store them in a sterilized jar in the refrigerator for up to 3 weeks. Makes 500 g (1 lb 2 oz)

spiced nuts

Preheat the oven to 170°C (325°F/Gas 3). Put 1 teaspoon each of cumin seeds, coriander seeds, mustard seeds and ground turmeric in a spice grinder or small blender with 1/4 teaspoon fennel seeds, 1/2 cinnamon stick and 1/2 teaspoon black peppercorns and grind to a fine powder. Transfer the mixture to a large bowl and add 2 tablespoons soft brown sugar, 1 tablespoon finely grated orange zest, 2 teaspoons sea salt and 100 g (3 1/2 oz/about 2/3 cup) each of pecans, peanuts, cashew nuts and macadamia nuts. Stir to combine, then add 2 tablespoons olive oil and mix well. Spread the nut mixture out on a baking tray. Bake, stirring occasionally, for 10–15 minutes, or until the nuts have coloured a little. Allow to cool completely. Store in an airtight container (for up to 2 weeks) until ready to serve. Makes 400 g (14 oz)

deep-fried whitebait

Rinse 500 g (1 lb 2 oz) whitebait under cold running water, then drain in a colander or large sieve. Put 125 g (4 1/2 oz/1 cup) plain (all-purpose) flour, 1 tablespoon sumac, 1/2 teaspoon cayenne pepper and 1 teaspoon sea salt in a large bowl and stir to mix well. Heat 750 ml (26 fl oz/3 cups) vegetable oil in a large deep saucepan until the surface begins to shimmer and a pinch of flour dropped into the oil fries immediately. Pat the whitebait dry with paper towels. Add the whitebait to the seasoned flour, tossing them until all the fish are well coated. With your fingers, lift them away from the bowl and shake free of any excess flour. Deep-fry the whitebait in batches for about 3 minutes, or until crisp and golden. Serve with a sprinkle of sea salt. Serves 4–6 as an appetizer

cherry bocconcini with a spice dip

Preheat the oven to 180°C (350°F/Gas 4). Cut 2 roma (plum) tomatoes into quarters and place them on a baking tray. Roast for 20 minutes, or until the tomatoes are beginning to dry out and blacken. Transfer to a food processor with 2 tablespoons lightly toasted sesame seeds, 1 tablespoon thyme leaves, 1 teaspoon sumac, 1 teaspoon sea salt, 1/2 teaspoon ground cumin and 1/4 teaspoon smoked paprika. Process to form a chunky paste, then spoon into a serving bowl alongside a pile of cherry bocconcini (fresh baby mozzarella cheese) — you'll need about 300 g (10 1/2 oz) bocconcini. Serves 4–6 as an appetizer.

potato and spinach frittata

400 g (14 oz) waxy potatoes, peeled
250 ml (9 fl oz/1 cup) vegetable stock (Basics)
3 tablespoons olive oil
1 red onion, diced
2 celery stalks, finely sliced
100 g (3 1/2 oz/2 1/4 cups) baby English spinach leaves
6 eggs, lightly beaten
70 g (2 1/2 oz/3/4 cup) grated parmesan cheese
green salad, to serve

Cut the potatoes into chunks approximately 1–2 cm (1/2–3/4 inch) square. Put the potato pieces in a deep frying pan and add the vegetable stock. Heat over high heat until most of the stock has evaporated, then reduce the heat to medium and add the oil, onion and celery and season with salt and pepper. Toss so that all the vegetables are lightly coated in the oil, then allow to cook for a few minutes until the vegetables are slightly softened.

Add the spinach leaves, stir for a few minutes until the leaves have wilted, then pour the beaten eggs over the top. Sprinkle with the parmesan and continue to cook for 10 minutes over medium heat until the egg is almost set. Remove from the heat and place under a grill (broiler) until the cheese is golden and the frittata has begun to puff up. Serve warm with a green salad. Serves 4–6

vegetable platter with two dips

beetroot dip
4 beetroot (beets) (about 150 g/5 1/2 oz each), washed but not peeled
4 thyme sprigs
250 g (9 oz/1 cup) plain yoghurt
1 teaspoon pomegranate molasses

herb dip
1 egg yolk
1/4 teaspoon sugar
1 handful flat-leaf (Italian) parsley
10 mint leaves
10 basil leaves
1 tablespoon lemon juice
125 ml (4 fl oz/1/2 cup) olive oil

mixed plate of crudités, such as radishes, baby carrots, fennel, cucumber and zucchini (courgettes)

To make the beetroot dip, preheat the oven to 200°C (400°F/Gas 6). Put the beetroot in a roasting tin with the thyme sprigs and 250 ml (9 fl oz/1 cup) of water. Cover with foil and bake for 1 hour, or until the beetroot is cooked and tender when pierced with a skewer. Wearing rubber gloves to stop your hands staining, peel the skins from the beetroot — they should slip free quite easily. Roughly chop the flesh, then put the flesh in a food processor and blend to a smooth paste. Transfer to a bowl and stir in the yoghurt and pomegranate molasses. Season to taste with sea salt and a generous grind of black pepper.

To make the herb dip, place the egg yolk, sugar, herbs and lemon juice in a blender and blend to a purée. Pour into a bowl and slowly whisk in the oil until it forms a creamy mayonnaise. Season with sea salt and freshly ground black pepper.

Serve the dips with a plate of crudités. Serves 4–6

a warm pan of eggs, cheese and golden potato

Opposite: potato and spinach frittata
Over: vegetable platter with two dips

PRODUCE
RED RIVER
PRODUCE OF TURKEY
MALATYA - TÜRKİYE
KAMBARA
CITRUS
KAMBARA CITRUS
KAMBARA PTY. LTD.
CITRUS
CHEMICAL FREE
CAUTION

hummus

400 g (14 oz) tin chickpeas, drained and rinsed
2 teaspoons ground cumin
juice of 1 lemon
3 tablespoons tahini
3 tablespoons extra virgin olive oil
ground cumin, extra, to serve
extra virgin olive oil, extra, to serve

Put the chickpeas, cumin, lemon juice, tahini and oil in a food processor and blend until you have a chunky purée, adding several tablespoons of warm water to reach a smooth consistency. Spoon into a serving bowl, sprinkle with a little extra cumin and some pepper, then drizzle with a little more olive oil. Serves 4

eggplant and mozzarella salad

2 eggplants (aubergines)
2 roasted red capsicums (peppers), seeds, membranes and skin removed (Basics)
vegetable oil, for frying
1 buffalo mozzarella or 4 bocconcini (fresh baby mozzarella cheese)
2 tablespoons pine nuts, toasted
10 large basil leaves
2 tablespoons extra virgin olive oil
1 tablespoon balsamic vinegar

Slice the eggplants into 5 mm (1/4 inch) thick rounds and place in a colander. Sprinkle liberally with sea salt and leave for 1 hour.

Slice the capsicums into thick strips. Rinse the eggplant and drain well on paper towels. Fry the eggplant rounds in vegetable oil over medium–high heat until golden brown on both sides — you will probably need to do this in batches. Drain on paper towels.

Arrange the eggplant slices over a platter and top with the capsicum strips, torn pieces of the mozzarella, pine nuts and basil leaves. Season lightly with sea salt and pepper. In a small bowl combine the extra virgin olive oil and vinegar and stir to blend. Spoon over the salad. Serves 4–6 as a starter or side dish

eggplant dip

2 eggplants (aubergines)
1 small garlic clove, finely chopped
100 g (3 1/2 oz) plain yoghurt
juice of 1 lemon
2 tablespoons tahini
1 handful flat-leaf (Italian) parsley, roughly chopped
1/2 teaspoon ground cumin
pinch of ground white pepper
2 tablespoons pine nuts, toasted
ciabatta bread, lightly toasted, to serve

Prick the eggplants all over with a fork, then sit them directly on the naked flame of a gas burner or over a barbecue. Set the flames to low–medium and cook for 10 minutes, turning them occasionally. Cook until the eggplants are blackened and blistered and beginning to collapse. (If you don't have a gas stove you can do this in the oven. Lightly rub the eggplants in oil, then cook in a preheated 200°C (400°F/Gas 6) oven until the skins begin to blister and blacken — you may need to turn them several times so the skins blister all over.)

Remove from the heat and place into a bowl. Cover with plastic wrap. Allow the eggplants to cool, then gently peel away the blackened skin. Put the flesh in a colander or sieve over a large bowl and leave to drain for 5 minutes.

Mix the garlic with the yoghurt, then add the eggplant pulp, lemon juice, tahini and parsley. Stir the mixture thoroughly, breaking up the eggplant as you go. Season with the cumin, a little sea salt and white pepper. Spoon into a serving bowl, sprinkle with the pine nuts and serve with lightly toasted ciabatta. Serves 4

crispy bread, bowls of flavour and a dash of spice

Opposite: hummus
Over: eggplant and mozzarella salad; eggplant dip

bread salad with fried sardines

3 ripe tomatoes, diced
1 Lebanese (short) cucumber, diced
1 garlic clove, finely chopped
1 red chilli, seeded and finely chopped
1 handful flat leaf (Italian) parsley, roughly chopped
4 basil leaves, finely sliced
2 tablespoons red wine vinegar
4 slices sourdough, lightly toasted
1 tablespoon butter
8–16 fresh sardine fillets, depending on their size

In a large bowl combine the tomato, cucumber, garlic, chilli, parsley and basil. Pour over the vinegar. Tear the bread into small pieces and add it to the salad. Season with sea salt and freshly ground black pepper and toss to combine. Spoon the salad onto a large serving platter or divide among four plates.

Put a large non-stick frying pan over high heat and melt the butter. Fry the sardine fillets for 1–2 minutes on both sides or until they are opaque and slightly browned. Remove and lay over the salad. Serves 4

oysters with a sherry dressing

1 tablespoon dry sherry
1 tablespoon lime juice
1/2 teaspoon fish sauce
1/4 teaspoon sesame oil
1 teaspoon soft brown sugar
1 spring onion (scallion), green part finely sliced
24 small oysters

Combine the sherry, lime juice, fish sauce, sesame oil and sugar in a small bowl and stir to combine. Add the spring onion to the dressing just before serving.

Serve the oysters with a drizzle of the dressing or allow your guests to help themselves. Serves 4

buttery fried sardines, fresh herbs and a chilli bite

Opposite: bread salad with fried sardines
Over: oysters with a sherry dressing

italian white bean and tuna dip

400 g (14 oz) tin cannellini (white) beans, drained and rinsed
3 tablespoons extra virgin olive oil
1 tablespoon lemon juice
95 g (3 1/4 oz) tin tuna in oil, drained
1 handful flat-leaf (Italian) parsley, chopped
8 kalamata olives, pitted and finely chopped
extra virgin olive oil, extra, for drizzling
pide (Turkish/flat bread), toasted, to serve

Place the cannellini beans, oil, lemon juice and tuna in a food processor and pulse several times so that the beans are broken up but not mashed. Scoop into a bowl and fold in the parsley and olives. Drizzle with a little extra virgin olive oil. Serve with toasted fingers of pide. Serves 4–6

prosciutto with braised fennel and zucchini

2 fennel bulbs
3 tablespoons olive oil
juice of 1 lemon
2 zucchini (courgettes)
6 thin slices of prosciutto
10 mint leaves, torn

Preheat the oven to 200°C (400°F/Gas 6). Line a baking tin with baking paper. Trim the fennel, reserving any of the feathery green tops and cut the bulbs into eighths lengthways. Place the pieces in the baking tin and pour over the oil and 1 tablespoon of the lemon juice. Season the fennel with sea salt and freshly ground black pepper. Cover the tin with foil and bake for 30 minutes. Remove the tin from the oven and allow the fennel to cool a little.

Slice the zucchini into long thin ribbons using a vegetable peeler. Tear the prosciutto into small thin strips. Arrange the fennel, zucchini slices and prosciutto over a serving platter and scatter with torn mint leaves and some fronds of fennel greens. Pour over the cooking juices from the fennel and drizzle with the remaining lemon juice. Serves 4 as a side dish

a mouthful of mediterranean flavours

Opposite: italian white bean and tuna dip
Over: prosciutto with braised fennel and zucchini

red capsicum, anchovy and egg salad

4 organic eggs, at room temperature
3 roasted red capsicums (peppers), seeds, membranes and skin removed (Basics)
3 tablespoons extra virgin olive oil
1 teaspoon balsamic vinegar
8 radicchio leaves
100 g (3$^1/_2$ oz/3 cups) wild rocket (arugula) leaves
1 tablespoon salted capers, rinsed and drained
8 good-quality anchovy fillets
1 handful flat-leaf (Italian) parsley

Bring a saucepan of water to the boil and add the eggs. Boil the eggs for 5 minutes, then remove them from the pan and allow to cool.

Cut or tear the roasted capsicum flesh into long strips. Place the capsicum strips into a bowl, add the oil and vinegar, then season with sea salt and freshly ground black pepper. Toss to ensure the capsicum strips are well coated in the dressing.

Tear the radicchio leaves in half and arrange them over a serving platter, then top with the rocket and dressed capsicum, reserving the marinating mixture in the bowl. Peel the eggs, then cut them in half and add them to the salad. Scatter with the capers, anchovies and parsley. Drizzle with any of the remaining capsicum oil and serve. Serves 4

red capsicum, anchovy and egg salad

prosciutto and beetroot salad

2 ripe roma (plum) tomatoes, diced
1/2 red onion, diced
1 Lebanese (short) cucumber, diced
1 tablespoon salted capers, rinsed and drained
1 teaspoon red wine vinegar
8 slices of prosciutto, cut in half
1 large beetroot (beet), peeled and grated
2 hard-boiled eggs, grated
2 tablespoons finely chopped curly parsley
3 tablespoons extra virgin olive oil
sourdough or crispbread, to serve

Put the diced tomatoes, onion, cucumber, capers and red wine vinegar into a bowl and toss together.

Arrange the prosciutto over a round serving platter and top with the grated beetroot, allowing a little of the prosciutto to be seen around the edges. Spoon the tomato salad over the beetroot, then top with the grated egg. Sprinkle with the parsley, season with freshly ground black pepper and drizzle with the olive oil. Serve with thin slices of sourdough or crispbread. Serves 4

roast lamb with fresh mint aïoli

30 g (1 oz/1 bunch) rosemary
1.5 kg (3 lb 5 oz) leg of lamb
2 tablespoons olive oil
cooked waxy potatoes, to serve

aïoli
1 egg yolk
1 garlic clove, roughly chopped
1 tablespoon white wine vinegar
125 ml (4 fl oz/1/2 cup) olive oil
30 mint leaves, finely chopped

Preheat the oven to 200°C (400°F/Gas 6). Scatter the rosemary over the base of a roasting tin, then sit the leg of lamb on top. Rub the surface of the lamb with a little olive oil, then rub sea salt and pepper into the skin. Place in the preheated oven. After 30 minutes remove the lamb and spoon some of the roasting juices over the meat. Return to the oven for a further 40 minutes. Transfer the lamb to a warmed serving plate and cover with foil. Allow the meat to rest for 15 minutes before carving.

While the lamb is resting, make the aïoli. Put the egg yolk in a small food processor with the garlic and vinegar. Blend, then pour the mixture into a large bowl. Slowly whisk in the oil until you have a thick mayonnaise. Stir in the mint leaves and enough warm water to make the aïoli the consistency of a thin sauce.

Carve the lamb and serve with the fresh mint aïoli and boiled potatoes. Serves 6

a salad of fresh earthy flavours to share with friends

Opposite: prosciutto and beetroot salad
Over: roast lamb with fresh mint aïoli

salad of duck, fennel and watercress

1 whole Chinese roasted duck
1 large fennel bulb, shaved
4 handfuls picked watercress sprigs
3 tablespoons dry sherry
juice of 1 orange
1 tablespoon soy sauce
1 teaspoon sesame oil
1 teaspoon sugar
1 heaped tablespoon small salted capers, rinsed and drained

Preheat the oven to 160°C (315°F/Gas 2–3). Remove the skin from the duck and, using a pair of kitchen scissors, cut the skin into thin strips. Put the strips on a baking tray and into the hot oven for 10 minutes, or until the skin starts to become crisp. Remove and drain on paper towels. Pull the flesh from the duck and roughly shred it. Place the duck flesh and crispy pieces of skin into a large bowl and add the shaved fennel and half the watercress.

In a small bowl combine the sherry, orange juice, soy sauce, sesame oil and sugar. Stir until the sugar has dissolved, then drizzle over the salad. Arrange the remaining watercress on a serving platter or in a bowl and top with the duck salad. Toss lightly, then sprinkle with the capers. Serves 4

a wok of aromatic mussels

2 kg (4 lb 8 oz) mussels
1 1/2 tablespoons unsalted butter
2 slices of prosciutto, finely chopped
1 celery stalk, finely sliced
2 spring onions (scallions), finely sliced
250 ml (9 fl oz/1 cup) dry white wine
1 handful flat-leaf (Italian) parsley, roughly chopped
crusty bread and green salad, to serve

Clean the mussels in the sink under cold running water, scrubbing them to remove any barnacles or bits of hairy 'beard'. Throw away any broken mussels, or open ones that don't close when you tap them.

Place a large wok over low heat and add the butter, prosciutto, celery and spring onion. Cook for 7 minutes, or until the onion and celery are soft. Add the white wine and bring to the boil. Add the mussels and cover with a lid or foil. Cook for several minutes, shaking the wok several times to ensure the heat is reaching all the mussels. Remove the lid and check that all the mussels have opened. If not, toss them once more and return to the heat for a further minute. Throw away any mussels that haven't opened, then scatter the rest with the chopped parsley.

Ladle the mussels into deep bowls, ensuring that lots of the juices from the wok are included, and serve with a loaf of crusty bread and a green salad. Serves 4

Opposite: salad of duck, fennel and watercress
Over: a wok of aromatic mussels

spring greens with a lemon butter sauce

Bring a large saucepan of salted water to the boil. Trim 350 g (12 oz/2 bunches) asparagus, 200 g (7 oz) green beans and 200 g (7 oz) sugar snap peas and set aside. Heat 1 tablespoon lemon juice in a small saucepan over low heat and add $2^{1}/_{2}$ tablespoons chilled butter. Pierce the butter with a fork and slowly stir the butter into the lemon juice. When all the butter has melted it should have formed a smooth buttery sauce. Remove from the heat and set to the back of the stove where it will remain warm while the vegetables are being cooked. Add the vegetables to the pan of boiling water and blanch for a few minutes, or until they have all turned dark green. Drain and arrange them over a warmed serving plate. Drizzle with the lemon butter sauce and season with sea salt and freshly ground black pepper. Serve with fish or chicken. Serves 4–6 as a side dish

baby beets with a walnut dressing

Preheat the oven to 180°C (350°F/Gas 4). Cut the leafy tops from 625 g (1 lb 6 oz/1 bunch) small beetroot (beets) and rinse and reserve any of the smaller tender leaves. Place the bulbs in a roasting tin and add 250 ml (9 fl oz/1 cup) water. Cover with foil and bake for 1 hour, or until the beetroot are cooked through. Allow to cool. Rub the skins away from the beetroot wearing rubber gloves to prevent your hands from staining. Slice the beetroot into halves and put into a bowl. In a smaller bowl combine 2 tablespoons walnut oil, 1 tablespoon balsamic vinegar and 1 teaspoon honey. Stir until the honey has dissolved, then pour over the beetroot. Season, then toss well. Arrange 150 g ($5^{1}/_{2}$ oz/1 bunch) rocket (arugula) leaves on a platter, then add the beetroot. Scatter with 50 g ($1^{3}/_{4}$ oz/$^{1}/_{3}$ cup) roasted cashew nuts and the small beetroot leaves. Serve with veal cutlets or chargrilled beef. Serves 4 as a side dish

spring greens and roast capsicum

Bring a large saucepan of water to the boil and add 500 g (1 lb 2 oz/2 bunches) broccolini and 350 g (12 oz/ 2 1/4 cups) frozen broad (fava) beans. Cook for a few minutes, or until the broccolini is emerald green, then drain and rinse under cold water. When cool enough to handle, peel the outer skin from the broad beans, placing the small green beans into a bowl. Remove the seeds, membranes and skin from 4 roasted red capsicums (peppers) (Basics), then tear the flesh into strips. Put the strips into a bowl with 3 tablespoons extra virgin olive oil and 1 tablespoon balsamic vinegar. Season with sea salt and freshly ground black pepper and toss so that the capsicum is well coated in the dressing. Arrange the broccolini on a serving platter and add the dressed capsicum, then scatter with the broad beans and serve with sausages or seared lamb. Serves 4 as a side dish

roast potatoes, tomatoes and olives

Preheat the oven to 200°C (400°F/Gas 6). Peel 1 kg (2 lb 4 oz) waxy potatoes and cut into bite-sized chunks. Put in a saucepan of cold water and bring to the boil. Simmer for 10 minutes, then drain. Pile the potato in a large roasting tin. In a small bowl combine 3 tablespoons olive oil, 2 tablespoons lemon juice and 2 tablespoons roughly chopped rosemary. Stir to combine, then pour over the potato. Season with sea salt and freshly ground black pepper and, using your hands, toss the potato a few times to ensure it is well coated. Bake for 10 minutes, then remove and turn the potato once. Return to the oven for 10 minutes, then remove once more and add 500 g (1 lb 2 oz/ 4 cups) cherry tomatoes and 20 kalamata olives. Return to the oven and cook for a further 15 minutes, or until the tomatoes are beginning to soften and split. Serve with roast chicken or lamb. Serves 4 as a side dish

baked fish with chilli sauce

70 g ($2^1/_2$ oz/$^1/_2$ cup) grated palm sugar or soft brown sugar
1 teaspoon chilli flakes
2 tablespoons lime juice
1 teaspoon fish sauce
2 lemon grass stems
2 spring onions (scallions)
125 ml (4 fl oz/$^1/_2$ cup) dry white wine
4 x 200 g (7 oz) thick blue-eye cod or barramundi fillets
2 tablespoons olive oil
1 handful coriander (cilantro) leaves
2 limes, cut into quarters

Preheat the oven to 180°C (350°F/Gas 4). To make the chilli sauce, put the sugar and 100 ml ($3^1/_2$ fl oz) of water in a small heavy-based saucepan. Bring to the boil, then boil for 3 minutes. Add the chilli flakes and take the pan off the heat. Allow to cool, then add the lime juice and fish sauce.

Cut the lemon grass and spring onions into 8 cm ($3^1/_4$ inch) lengths and put them in a roasting tin with the wine and 250 ml (9 fl oz/1 cup) of water. Rinse the fish fillets under cold running water and pat dry. Sprinkle with sea salt, then place on top of the lemon grass and spring onion. Drizzle the fish with the oil, cover with foil and bake for 25 minutes. To ensure that the flesh is cooked through, insert the tip of a knife into the thickest part of one of the fillets.

Lift the fish fillets onto a warmed platter (with the lemon grass and spring onion as garnish, if you like). Scatter with coriander and drizzle with the chilli sauce. Serve with lime wedges. Serves 4

pork spare ribs

250 ml (9 fl oz/1 cup) soy sauce
175 g (6 oz/$^1/_2$ cup) golden syrup or maple syrup
4 tablespoons balsamic vinegar
4 tablespoons tomato paste (concentrated purée)
juice of 1 orange, plus 1 strip of orange zest
1 tablespoon mustard powder
1 tablespoon finely grated fresh ginger
1 cinnamon stick
$^1/_2$ teaspoon ground cumin
$^1/_2$ teaspoon chilli powder
1 bay leaf
16–24 American-style pork ribs, no thicker than 2 cm ($^3/_4$ inch)
polenta or mashed pumpkin (Basics), to serve

Place all the ingredients except for the ribs into a small saucepan and bring to the boil, stirring to ensure that the marinade does not catch on the base of the saucepan. Remove the cinnamon stick and allow the marinade to cool a little. Pour over the ribs, ensuring that they are all well coated in the marinade. Cover and refrigerate for several hours or preferably overnight.

Preheat the oven to 200°C (400°F/Gas 6). Line an ovenproof ceramic baking dish with baking paper and arrange the ribs so they are lying flat. Pour over any of the remaining marinade. Bake for 30 minutes, turning once after 15 minutes. Remove to a serving plate and spoon over the juices from the baking dish. Serve with soft polenta or creamy mashed pumpkin. Serves 4

roast pork with soy-roasted pumpkin

1.5 kg (3 lb 5 oz) piece of pork shoulder
4 sage sprigs
1 kg (2 lb 4 oz) jap or kent pumpkin
3 tablespoons olive oil
1 tablespoon soy sauce
1 red chilli, seeded and finely chopped
$^1/_2$ teaspoon Chinese five-spice
steamed greens (Basics), to serve

Preheat the oven to 220°C (425°F/Gas 7). Ask your butcher to score the skin of the pork. Pat the pork dry with paper towels and rub the scored skin with a generous amount of salt. Season with freshly ground black pepper. Scatter the sage sprigs over the base of a roasting tin, then place the pork on top, skin side up. Cook for 25 minutes, then reduce the heat to 180°C (350°F/Gas 4) and cook for a further hour.

Meanwhile, peel the pumpkin and cut it into small chunks. Place the chunks in a large bowl and add the oil, soy sauce, chilli and five-spice. Toss well, then transfer to a baking tray. Add to the oven 30 minutes before the pork is due to be completely cooked. By this stage the pumpkin should be cooked and golden.

Remove the pork from the oven and reduce the heat to low to keep the pumpkin warm. To test if the meat is done insert a sharp knife or skewer into the centre – the juices should run clear. Transfer the pork to a warmed serving platter. If the skin needs further cooking remove it with a sharp knife and return it to the roasting tin and cook on the top shelf of the oven for a few minutes. Cover the pork with foil and allow to rest for 15 minutes before carving. Serve with the roast pumpkin and steamed greens. Serves 6

Opposite: baked fish with chilli sauce
Over: pork spare ribs; roast pork with soy-roasted pumpkin

nectarine clafoutis

400 g (14 oz) ripe nectarines, stones removed, cut into quarters
125 ml (4 fl oz/1/2 cup) pouring (whipping) cream
3 eggs
3 tablespoons caster (superfine) sugar
60 g (2 1/4 oz/1/2 cup) plain (all-purpose) flour
2 teaspoons natural vanilla extract
icing (confectioners') sugar, to serve
vanilla ice cream (Basics), to serve

Preheat the oven to 200°C (400°F/Gas 6). Lightly butter a 1 litre (35 fl oz/4 cup) ovenproof baking dish, then arrange the nectarines over the base with their skin side down.

Put the cream, eggs, caster sugar, flour and vanilla into a food processor and process to form a smooth batter. Pour over the nectarines and bake for 30 minutes, or until the clafoutis is puffed up and golden brown. Allow to cool a little before sprinkling with icing sugar and serving with vanilla ice cream. Serves 6

marsala-baked figs

8 figs
4 tablespoons soft brown sugar
1 1/2 tablespoons unsalted butter
125 ml (4 fl oz/1/2 cup) marsala
grated zest and juice of 1 lemon
4 tablespoons flaked or slivered almonds
mascarpone, to serve

Preheat the oven to 180°C (350°F/Gas 4). Slit a cross into the top of each fig and slice halfway down the figs, keeping them attached at the base. Sit them in an ovenproof ceramic baking dish and slightly open the figs at the top. Put a heaped teaspoon of sugar and some of the butter into the centre of each fig. Pour the marsala into the baking dish and add the lemon zest and juice along with the remaining butter and sugar. Bake for 10 minutes.

Put the almonds on a baking tray and toast in the oven for 2–3 minutes, or until golden brown.

Serve the figs with mascarpone, some toasted almonds and a drizzle of the baking liquids. Serves 4

serve warm from the oven with a dusting of suga

Opposite: nectarine clafoutis
Over: marsala-baked figs

FIGS

apple and rhubarb crumble

60 g (2 1/4 oz/1/2 cup) plain (all-purpose) flour
90 g (3 1/4 oz/1/2 cup) soft brown sugar
40 g (1 1/2 oz/1/2 cup) desiccated coconut
4 tablespoons unsalted butter, cut into cubes
400 g (14 oz/1 bunch) rhubarb, rinsed
3 small green apples
3 tablespoons caster (superfine) sugar
thick (double/heavy) cream, custard (page 52) or vanilla ice cream (Basics), to serve

Preheat the oven to 150°C (300°F/Gas 2). To make the crumble topping, put the flour, brown sugar and coconut into a bowl. Add the butter and rub it into the dry ingredients until the mixture starts to look like breadcrumbs.

Cut the rhubarb into 2 cm (3/4 inch) lengths and place into a large bowl. Peel and roughly chop the apples into 2 cm (3/4 inch) cubes and add them to the rhubarb with the caster sugar. Toss several times to ensure that the fruit is well coated in the sugar, then place the fruit in a 1 litre (35 fl oz/4 cup) ovenproof ceramic baking dish. Flatten the fruit out, then top with the crumble mix. Bake for 1 1/2 hours, or until the top is golden and the fruit has cooked through. Serve warm with cream, custard or vanilla ice cream. Serves 4–6

apple and rhubarb crumble

summertime pavlova

3 eggs, separated
4 tablespoons caster (superfine) sugar
1/2 teaspoon white wine vinegar
1/4 teaspoon cream of tartar
1 teaspoon cornflour (cornstarch)
1 teaspoon natural vanilla extract
3 peaches, peeled and finely sliced
3 passionfruit
whipped cream, to serve

Preheat the oven to 150°C (300°F/Gas 2). Line a baking tray with baking paper. Beat the egg whites until soft peaks form. Gradually add the sugar, then the vinegar, cream of tartar, cornflour and vanilla extract and continue to beat to form stiff peaks. Spoon the meringue onto the centre of the tray, then spread it out to form a 20 cm (8 inch) circle. Put into the preheated oven for 15 minutes, then reduce the heat to 120°C (235°F/Gas 1/2) and bake for a further hour. Turn the oven off, leave the door slightly ajar and allow the meringue to completely cool in the oven.

Serve topped with sliced peaches, passionfruit and whipped cream. Serves 6

passionfruit jelly with lychees

400 g (14 oz) tin lychees
1 teaspoon lime juice
3 tablespoons caster (superfine) sugar
6 gelatine leaves or powdered gelatine (follow the manufacturer's instructions)
juice of 2 oranges
160 ml (5 1/4 fl oz) passionfruit juice
fresh lychees, to serve

Drain the lychees, reserving the lychee juice. Place the lychees into a bowl, cover with water and add the lime juice. Chill in the refrigerator until ready to serve.

Pour the reserved lychee juice into a saucepan with the sugar and heat over low heat, stirring until the sugar dissolves.

Soak the gelatine leaves in a large bowl of cold water for 5–10 minutes, or until very soft. Squeeze any excess liquid from the gelatine, then stir the gelatine into the warm lychee syrup. Pour the warm syrup into a measuring container, add the passionfruit juice and enough orange juice to make 600 ml (21 fl oz) of liquid. Stir to ensure that all the liquids are well combined, then pour the mixture into four 200 ml (7 fl oz) glasses and refrigerate for 3 hours or overnight, until set.

Drain the lychees, then serve with the passionfruit jelly (gelatine dessert). Serves 4

a soft pillow of meringue topped with sunny fruit

Opposite: summertime pavlova
Over: passionfruit jelly with lychees

pot

enamel and iron, shiny and worn,

old favourites and new friends

Warming...

Gather around a bubbling, straight-from-the-flame meaty casserole and catch the first billow of aromatic steam as the lid is removed. Relish meaty stews, simmered vegetables, fruity jams and poached fruit. The seductive magic of many flavours melding in one simple pot is what cooking is all about.

citrus curd

2 large lemons
1 mandarin
100 g (3 1/2 oz) unsalted butter
175 g (6 oz/heaped 3/4 cup) sugar
3 eggs yolks, beaten
whipped cream, to serve
brioche, sourdough, sponge cake or tartlet cases (Basics), to serve

Finely grate the zest of both lemons and the mandarin, then juice them and pass through a strainer. You should end up with 170 ml (5 1/2 fl oz/2/3 cup) juice.

In a heavy-based saucepan, combine the butter, citrus juice, grated zest and sugar. Stir constantly over medium heat until the sugar has dissolved. Remove the pan from the heat and whisk in the egg yolks. Return to the heat and continue to lightly whisk until the curd has begun to thicken, being careful not to bring it to the boil.

Pour the hot curd into a 300 ml (10 1/2 fl oz) sterilized jar and allow to cool. Seal with a lid and refrigerate until ready to use. This will keep for several weeks in the refrigerator. Serve with warm brioche, toasted sourdough or spooned over a sponge cake or tartlet cases and topped with whipped cream. Makes approximately 250 ml (9 fl oz/1 cup)

summer jam

200 g (7 oz/1 1/3 cups) strawberries, rinsed and hulled
2 ripe peaches (300 g/10 1/2 oz in total)
400 g (14 oz/heaped 1 3/4 cups) sugar
buttered toast, fresh scones (Basics) or sponge cake, to serve

Slice the strawberries in half and put them into a bowl. Remove the skin from the peaches and roughly slice the flesh into the bowl. Pour the sugar over the fruit and stir once or twice. Cover with plastic wrap and allow to marinate for 2 hours.

Put the fruit and sugar in a saucepan and bring to the boil before reducing to a low simmer. Remove any frothy scum that may come to the surface. Continue to simmer for 40 minutes, stirring occasionally.

Place several saucers in the freezer. Test that the jam is done by dropping a little jam onto a cold saucer and returning to the freezer for 1 minute. When the jam begins to form a skin it is ready.

Pour the jam into a 300 ml (10 1/2 fl oz) sterilized jar and allow to cool. Seal with a lid and refrigerate until ready to use. This will keep for several weeks in the refrigerator. Serve on buttered toast, fresh scones or spooned over a sponge cake. Makes approximately 250 ml (9 fl oz/1 cup)

a childhood memory of tangy, buttery smooth citrus

Opposite: citrus curd
Over: summer jam

Summer
2006

sweet couscous

1 orange
1 teaspoon butter
2–4 teaspoons honey, to taste
100 g (3 1/2 oz/1/2 cup) couscous
1/2 teaspoon ground cinnamon
50 g (1 3/4 oz/1/3 cup) currants
50 g (1 3/4 oz/1/2 cup) pecans, roughly chopped
400 g (14 oz) plain yoghurt

Grate the orange until you have 1 teaspoon zest, then juice the orange.

Pour 100 ml (3 1/2 fl oz) of water into a saucepan and add the butter, honey and orange juice. Bring to the boil, then pour in the couscous. Stir once or twice, then remove the pan from the heat and cover with a lid. Allow the couscous to remain covered for 10 minutes, then fluff with a fork. Keep covered until the couscous has cooled completely.

Add the cinnamon, currants, pecans and grated orange zest to the couscous. Stir well, then divide among four bowls and top with yoghurt. Serves 4

tomato and chilli jam

5 large red chillies
100 ml (3 1/2 fl oz) olive oil
1 teaspoon cumin seeds
1 teaspoon mustard seeds
1 teaspoon ground turmeric
1 teaspoon finely grated fresh ginger
4 garlic cloves, finely chopped
1 kg (2 lb 4 oz) ripe tomatoes, roughly chopped
125 g (4 1/2 oz/heaped 1/2 cup) sugar
100 ml (3 1/2 fl oz) white wine vinegar
1 tablespoon fish sauce
fried eggs, roast beef, grilled pork or barbecued sausages, to serve

Slice the chillies in half and remove most of the seeds. Finely slice the flesh into long thin strips.

Pour the oil into a heavy-based saucepan over medium heat and add the cumin seeds, mustard seeds, turmeric and grated ginger. When the mustard seeds begin to pop, add the garlic and chilli strips, stir a few times, then add the chopped tomatoes, sugar, vinegar and fish sauce. Bring to the boil, then reduce the heat and simmer, stirring occasionally, for 2 hours, or until the jam has thickened.

Pour the jam into a sterilized 500 ml (17 fl oz/2 cup) jar and allow to cool. Seal with a lid and refrigerate until ready to use. This will keep for several weeks in the refrigerator. Serve with fried eggs, roast beef, grilled pork or barbecued sausages. Makes 500 ml (17 fl oz/2 cups)

sweetly spiced grains, yoghurt and morning sunshine

Opposite: sweet couscous
Over: tomato and chilli jam

lentil and pumpkin salad

lentil and pumpkin salad

1 kg (2 lb 4 oz) jap or kent pumpkin
1 large red onion
2 tablespoons olive oil
120 g (4 1/4 oz/2/3 cup) puy lentils or tiny blue-green lentils
1/2 teaspoon sea salt
1 teaspoon wholegrain mustard
1 tablespoon balsamic vinegar
2 tablespoons extra virgin olive oil
1 handful flat-leaf (Italian) parsley, roughly chopped
50 g (1 3/4 oz/1 1/2 cups) wild rocket (arugula) leaves
100 g (3 1/2 oz) goat's cheese

Preheat the oven to 180°C (350°F/Gas 4). Peel the pumpkin and remove any seeds. Cut the pumpkin flesh into bite-sized chunks and place them on a baking tray. Peel the onion and cut it in half before slicing it into small half moons. Scatter the onion pieces over the pumpkin. Drizzle with the olive oil and season with a little sea salt and freshly ground black pepper. Bake for about 25 minutes, or until the pumpkin is cooked through and the onion is starting to blacken a little on the ends.

Meanwhile, put the lentils in a small saucepan with the salt and 500 ml (17 fl oz/2 cups) of water. Bring to the boil, then simmer for 30 minutes, or until tender. Drain the lentils of any excess water, then stir in the mustard, vinegar, extra virgin olive oil and parsley.

Arrange the rocket leaves on a serving plate, top with the pumpkin and onion, then spoon over the lentils. Crumble the goat's cheese over the top and serve. Serves 4

poached tomato salad

4 large vine-ripened tomatoes
8 peppercorns
2 teaspoons sea salt
1 tablespoon balsamic vinegar
1/2 red onion, finely sliced
70 g (2 1/2 oz/1/2 bunch) flat-leaf (Italian) parsley
1 handful wild rocket (arugula) leaves
8 basil leaves, roughly torn
150 g (5 1/2 oz/heaped 2/3 cup) drained and finely sliced marinated artichoke hearts
70 g (2 1/2 oz/3/4 cup) shaved pecorino cheese
2 tablespoons extra virgin olive oil
crusty bread, to serve

Preheat the oven to 180°C (350°F/Gas 4). Put the tomatoes in a small ovenproof ceramic baking dish, then fill the dish with enough water to come halfway up the tomatoes. Add the peppercorns, salt, vinegar, onion and 6 parsley sprigs to the dish. Put the dish in the oven and bake for 40 minutes.

Lift the tomatoes out of the dish with a slotted spoon and place them in the centre of four serving plates, reserving the cooking liquid. Arrange the rocket, basil and a few parsley leaves around the outside of the tomatoes. Top with the sliced artichoke hearts, then scatter with the pecorino. Drizzle each of the salads with some of the cooking liquid and a little extra virgin olive oil. Serve with crusty bread. Serves 4

artichoke and avocado salad

3 lemons, cut in half
4 artichokes
3 tablespoons extra virgin olive oil
8 mint leaves, finely chopped
1 handful flat-leaf (Italian) parsley, roughly chopped
1 garlic clove, crushed
2 avocados, diced
1 fennel bulb, shaved

Bring a large saucepan of salted water to the boil. Fill a large bowl with cold water and add the juice of 1 of the lemons to it. Taking 1 artichoke at a time, trim the artichoke stalks to within 2 cm (3/4 inch) of the artichoke head, then keep pulling away and discarding the outer leaves until you reach leaves with a base that looks yellow and crisp. Using a sharp knife, slice away the top third of the artichoke, then rub the artichoke with the cut side of a lemon. Place it in the bowl of lemon water and continue to trim the remaining artichokes. Remove the artichokes from the water and scrape out the central choke and pull out any of the spiky inner leaves. Return to the water until ready to use.

When the water is boiling, add the artichokes, weigh them down with a plate and simmer for 20 minutes. Test that the artichokes are done by pushing the tip of a knife into each one just above the stem — they should feel tender. Drain the cooked artichokes upside down for a minute, then slice in half lengthways.

Put the artichokes in a large dish with the oil, herbs, garlic and juice from the remaining lemon halves. Season with a little sea salt and freshly ground black pepper and toss to ensure that the artichokes are well coated in the marinade. Allow to cool, then arrange on a platter, along with the avocado and shaved fennel. Pour over some of the artichoke marinade as a dressing. Season with sea salt and freshly ground black pepper. Serves 4–6 as a side dish

soak up the flavours of a gently cooked ripe tomat

Opposite: poached tomato salad
Over: artichoke and avocado salad

fish stew

3 tablespoons olive oil
500 g (1 lb 2 oz) snapper fillets, cut into 5 cm (2 inch) pieces
500 g (1 lb 2 oz) ling fillets, cut into 5 cm (2 inch) pieces
pinch of saffron threads
2 spring onions (scallions), finely sliced
250 ml (9 fl oz/1 cup) dry white wine
1 litre (35 fl oz/4 cups) fish stock (Basics)
2 celery stalks, finely sliced
400 g (14 oz) tin chopped tomatoes
100 g (3 1/2 oz/1/2 cup) long-grain white rice
1 teaspoon dried oregano
1 bay leaf
1 handful curly parsley, roughly chopped
1 lemon, cut in half
mashed potato (Basics), to serve (optional)

Heat the oil in a large heavy-based saucepan over medium heat. Working in batches, add the fish pieces and lightly cook them on both sides, removing the fish as it becomes opaque. Set to one side.

Add the saffron threads and spring onions to the hot saucepan, stir once or twice in the warm oil, then add the white wine. Allow to simmer for a minute before adding the fish stock, celery, chopped tomatoes, rice, oregano and bay leaf. Bring the liquid to the boil, then reduce the heat and allow to simmer for 20 minutes, or until the rice is cooked.

Just before serving, remove the bay leaf, then return the fish to the pan and stir in the parsley. Season to taste with sea salt and freshly ground black pepper. Just prior to serving add a squeeze of lemon juice. Serve as is or with creamy mashed potato. Serves 4–6

bean and sausage stew

2 x 400 g (14 oz) tins cannellini (white) beans, drained and rinsed
5 ripe roma (plum) tomatoes, roughly chopped
400 g (14 oz) tin chopped tomatoes
2 leeks, rinsed and roughly chopped
6 garlic cloves, peeled
2 bay leaves
250 ml (9 fl oz/1 cup) dry white wine
350 g (12 oz) good-quality spicy, thick sausages
1 handful curly parsley, roughly chopped
mashed potato (Basics) or warm crusty bread, to serve

Preheat the oven to 180°C (350°F/Gas 4). Put the beans, fresh and tinned tomatoes, leek, garlic, bay leaves and white wine into a 3 litre (104 fl oz/12 cup) casserole dish or ovenproof pan. Season with a little sea salt and freshly ground black pepper.

Prick the skins of the sausages with a fork, then sear them in a non-stick frying pan over high heat until they are browned on all sides. Cut the sausages into bite-sized pieces and put them in the casserole dish. Lightly stir everything together, then cover the dish with a lid or foil and bake for 1 1/2 hours. Sprinkle with parsley and serve with creamy mashed potato or warm crusty bread. Serves 4

a hearty pot filled with the flavours of the sea

Opposite: fish stew
Over: bean and sausage stew

potted jerusalem artichokes with crisp-skinned snapper

3 tablespoons butter, melted
1 tablespoon lemon juice
500 g (1 lb 2 oz) Jerusalem artichokes, peeled
4 x 200 g (7 oz) snapper fillets
2 tablespoons olive oil
green salad, to serve

Preheat the oven to 180°C (350°F/Gas 4). Cut out six circles of baking paper that are the same size as the base of six standard muffin holes and use them to line the bases of a six-hole muffin tin.

Put the melted butter and lemon juice into a small bowl, add a little sea salt and pepper and stir to combine. Brush some of the butter over the baking paper and around the sides of the muffin holes.

Cut the Jerusalem artichokes into very thin slices and layer them in the muffin holes, brushing with the butter as you go. When all the holes have been filled, brush the final layer with butter, then cover with foil. Place into the oven and bake for 1 hour. Remove from the oven and allow to cool a little before tipping out onto a baking tray. Reduce the oven temperature to 150°C (300°F/Gas 2) and keep the artichokes, covered in foil, in the oven until ready to serve.

Rinse the fish fillets and pat dry with paper towels. Heat a non-stick frying pan over high heat and add the oil. Season the fish with sea salt, then sear the fillets, skin side down, for 1–2 minutes, or until the skin is crisp and golden. Lift the fish onto an ovenproof tray, skin side up, and bake for 8 minutes. Remove and place the snapper onto four warmed serving plates. Serve with a green salad and the potted artichokes. Serves 4

potted jerusalem artichokes with crisp-skinned snapper

linguine and prawns with roast chilli oil

chilli oil
4 large red chillies
150 ml (5 fl oz) olive oil

400 g (14 oz) linguine
1 tablespoon olive oil
2 garlic cloves, finely chopped
16 raw king prawns (shrimp), peeled and deveined
70 g (2 1/2 oz/2 cups) wild rocket (arugula) leaves
25 g (1 oz/1 bunch) chives, finely snipped
juice of 1 lemon

Preheat the oven to 150°C (300°F/Gas 2). To make the chilli oil, slice the chillies in half lengthways and remove some of the seeds if you like — the more seeds you leave intact the hotter the chilli oil will be. Place the chillies on a baking tray and bake for 10 minutes, or until the edges are beginning to curl up and darken.

Remove the chillies from the oven, roughly chop them, then put in a small food processor with the oil and blend several times until the chilli has completely broken down. Line a sieve with muslin (cheesecloth) and place it over a bowl. Pour the chilli oil into the sieve and allow the pure oil to drain into the bowl. The result is a rich red oil with a hint of a chilli bite.

Bring a large saucepan of salted water to the boil and cook the pasta until *al dente*.

Meanwhile, heat the olive oil in a frying pan over medium heat. Stir in the garlic, then add the prawns. Fry the prawns for 2–3 minutes, or until they are pink on both sides and have begun to curl up. Remove from the heat. Drain the linguine and return it to the pan. Add 4 tablespoons of the chilli oil, the prawns, rocket, chives and lemon juice. Toss well and season with a little sea salt. Pile into four warmed pasta bowls and drizzle with a little more of the chilli oil. Serves 4

soft polenta with rich tomato and olive sauce

2 tablespoons butter
1 red onion, diced
2 garlic cloves, finely chopped
1 tablespoon thyme leaves
900 g (2 lb) ripe roma (plum) tomatoes, diced
125 ml (4 fl oz/1/2 cup) red wine
10 kalamata olives, pitted and finely chopped
1 teaspoon sea salt
250 g (9 oz/1 2/3 cups) polenta
150 g (5 1/2 oz/1 1/2 cups) grated parmesan cheese
100 g (3 1/2 oz) butter, extra
1 handful basil

Heat the butter in a heavy-based saucepan over medium heat and add the onion, garlic and thyme. Cook until the onion is soft, then add the diced tomatoes, red wine and olives. Bring to the boil, then reduce the heat and allow the sauce to simmer for 1 hour, stirring occasionally.

Meanwhile, to cook the polenta, bring 1.5 litres (52 fl oz/6 cups) of water to the boil. Add the salt, then slowly pour in the polenta while whisking. Reduce the heat to low and cook for 40 minutes at a gentle simmer, stirring from time to time. Add the parmesan and extra butter and stir until incorporated.

Spoon the polenta into four warmed pasta bowls, smoothing it out and making a well in the centre. Add the tomato sauce and top with a scattering of basil leaves and a grind of black pepper. Serves 4

eggplant and chickpea stew

4–6 tablespoons olive oil
2 red onions, diced
2 garlic cloves, finely chopped
1 teaspoon ground cumin
1/2 teaspoon paprika
1 red capsicum (pepper), cut into 1 cm (1/2 inch) squares
2 zucchini (courgettes), thickly sliced
1 eggplant (aubergine), cut into 1 cm (1/2 inch) cubes
4 roma (plum) tomatoes, cut into 1 cm (1/2 inch) cubes
125 ml (4 fl oz/1/2 cup) red wine
400 g (14 oz) tin chickpeas, drained and rinsed
100 g (3 1/2 oz/2 1/4 cups) baby English spinach leaves
extra virgin olive oil, to serve

Heat a heavy-based saucepan over medium heat, add 2 tablespoons of the olive oil and the onion, garlic, cumin and paprika. Cook for 1 minute, then add the capsicum and zucchini. Cook for a few minutes until the vegetables are just soft and the zucchini is golden. Remove all the vegetables with a slotted spoon and set to one side.

Add 2 tablespoons of the oil to the pan and, when hot, add the eggplant. Cook, stirring occasionally, until the eggplant turns golden brown, adding the remaining oil if necessary. Add the tomato and wine and reduce the heat to a simmer. Cover and cook for 10 minutes. Add the zucchini, capsicum, chickpeas and spinach and season well, then cook for a further 2 minutes. Divide among four bowls and serve with a drizzle of extra virgin olive oil. Serves 4

Opposite: linguine and prawns with roast chilli oil
Over: soft polenta with rich tomato and olive sauce; eggplant and chickpea stew

poached chicken salad

90 g (3 1/4 oz/1 bunch) coriander (cilantro)
4 spring onions (scallions), 2 left whole, 2 roughly chopped
1 tablespoon sea salt
2 boneless, skinless chicken breasts
2–3 roasted red capsicums (peppers), seeds, membranes and skin removed, torn into strips (Basics)
4 tablespoons olive oil
1 tablespoon balsamic vinegar
1/2 teaspoon smoked paprika
1 telegraph (long) cucumber, peeled and diced
steamed couscous (Basics), to serve

Fill a large saucepan with water. Add some coriander sprigs, the whole spring onions and the salt. Bring to the boil. Add the chicken breasts to the boiling water, cover with a lid and turn off the heat. Allow to sit, covered, for 40 minutes.

Put the capsicum strips into a bowl with the oil, vinegar and paprika and season well with sea salt and freshly ground black pepper. Toss so that everything is well combined. Pick off the coriander leaves from the sprigs and add a handful of them to the bowl along with the cucumber and chopped spring onions.

Remove the chicken from the pan and finely slice them against the grain. Add the warm chicken to the capsicum salad and toss to combine. Serve with steamed couscous. Serves 4

lamb curry

1 kg (2 lb 4 oz) lamb shoulder, trimmed and cut into cubes
3 tablespoons olive oil
juice of 2 lemons
1 tablespoon finely grated fresh ginger
2 teaspoons garam masala
2 onions, finely sliced
400 g (14 oz) tin chopped tomatoes
2 tablespoons tomato paste (concentrated purée)
3 green chillies, seeded and cut into strips
250 ml (9 fl oz/1 cup) veal or beef stock (Basics)
10 mint leaves, finely chopped
300 g (10 1/2 oz) plain yoghurt
steamed white rice (Basics), to serve

Put the lamb cubes into a large ceramic dish and add 2 tablespoons of the oil, the lemon juice, ginger and garam masala. Massage the ingredients into the lamb to ensure it is well coated. Cover with plastic wrap and allow to marinate for 3 hours in the refrigerator.

Heat the remaining oil in a large heavy-based saucepan and add the onion. Cook for a few minutes until the onion is soft, then add the lamb — depending on the size of your pan you may need to cook the lamb in batches. Cook for several minutes until browned. Add the tomato, tomato paste, chilli and stock and return the rest of the lamb to the pan if necessary. Allow to simmer, stirring occasionally, over low heat for 1 1/2 hours, or until the liquid has reduced and the lamb is coated in a rich, thick sauce.

Meanwhile, stir the mint leaves into the yoghurt. Serve the lamb spooned over steamed rice with a dollop of minty yoghurt. Serves 4

beef in red wine

1 kg (2 lb 4 oz) stewing beef
1 tablespoon plain (all-purpose) flour
350 g (12 oz) pork belly
3 tablespoons olive oil
2 garlic cloves, finely chopped
1 leek, rinsed and finely diced
1 carrot, peeled and diced
2 celery stalks, finely sliced
400 g (14 oz) tin chopped tomatoes
500 ml (17 fl oz/2 cups) red wine
2 bay leaves
500 g (1 lb 2 oz) small French shallots or baby onions, peeled but left whole
mashed potato (Basics), to serve

Preheat the oven to 180°C (350°F/Gas 4). Trim the beef and cut it into bite-sized pieces. Put the beef pieces in a large bowl and add the flour and a grind of black pepper. Rub the pepper and flour into the beef, then set to one side.

Remove the rind from the pork belly and finely chop the rind and the flesh. Heat a 3 litre (104 fl oz/12 cup) flameproof casserole dish over high heat, add the oil and fry the pork for a few minutes, then add the garlic, leek, carrot and celery. Reduce the heat to low and cook for 10 minutes, or until the leek is soft. Remove all the ingredients with a slotted spoon, ensuring that most of the oil remains in the dish.

Increase the heat and add the beef (in batches if necessary) and cook until it has browned all over. Return the pork and vegetable mixture (and the rest of the beef if necessary) to the dish and add the tomato, red wine, bay leaves and shallots. Stir once or twice, then cover and bake for 1 1/2 hours. Season to taste with sea salt and freshly ground black pepper. If after this time the mixture is quite wet, remove the lid, otherwise keep the lid on. Cook for a further 30 minutes until the stew has a rich, thick sauce. Serve with creamy mashed potato. Serves 4

Opposite: poached chicken salad
Over: lamb curry; beef in red wine

lemon and parmesan spaghettini

Bring a large saucepan of salted water to the boil and add the juice of 1 lemon. Cook 400 g (14 oz) spaghettini until *al dente*, then drain and return it to the warm pan. Meanwhile, heat 3 tablespoons olive oil in a large frying pan over medium heat, add 2 finely chopped garlic cloves and 2 rinsed and sliced leeks and sauté until the leek is soft and transparent. Season with a little freshly ground black pepper. Add the mixture to the pan with the pasta, then add the grated zest of 2 lemons, the juice of 1 lemon, 2 tablespoons rinsed and drained small salted capers, 1 handful flat-leaf (Italian) parsley, roughly chopped, and 25 g (1 oz/1 bunch) chives, finely snipped, stirring them into the pasta. Divide among four warmed pasta bowls and sprinkle with 70 g (2 1/2 oz/3/4 cup) grated parmesan cheese. Serves 4

chilli bacon penne

Bring a large saucepan of salted water to the boil. Cook 400 g (14 oz) penne until *al dente*, then drain and return it to the warm pan. Meanwhile, melt 3 tablespoons butter in a large frying pan over medium heat, add 1 diced red onion, 2 finely chopped garlic cloves and 2 seeded and finely chopped red chillies and sauté until the onion is soft and transparent. Add 3 chopped slices of bacon and cook for 2 minutes. Add 4 roughly chopped roma (plum) tomatoes, cover and allow to simmer over low heat for 10 minutes. Using a spoon, roughly break up the tomatoes, then season with sea salt and freshly ground black pepper. Add the tomato sauce to the pan with the pasta and stir over a low heat until it coats all the pasta. Divide among four warmed pasta bowls and sprinkle with 70 g (2 1/2 oz/3/4 cup) grated parmesan cheese and 8 roughly torn basil leaves. Serves 4

casareccia with tuna and tomato

Bring a large saucepan of salted water to the boil. Cook 400 g (14 oz) casareccia or penne until *al dente*. Meanwhile, drain a 185 g (6 1/2 oz) tin of tuna in oil and roughly flake the tuna into a large bowl. Add 3 roughly chopped ripe tomatoes, 3 tablespoons extra virgin olive oil, 1 tablespoon rinsed and drained small salted capers, 12 pitted and roughly chopped olives, 10 roughly torn basil leaves and 150 g (5 1/2 oz/1 bunch) roughly chopped rocket (arugula) leaves. Drain the cooked pasta and add it to the bowl. Toss so that all the ingredients are well combined, then divide among four warmed pasta bowls. Top with 70 g (2 1/2 oz/ 3/4 cup) shaved parmesan cheese and serve. Serves 4

pesto and goat's cheese linguine

Bring a large saucepan of salted water to the boil. Cook 400 g (14 oz) linguine until *al dente*, then drain and return to the warm pan. Add 4 heaped tablespoons pesto (Basics), 150 g (5 1/2 oz) crumbled goat's cheese and 50 g (1 3/4 oz/1 1/2 cups) wild rocket (arugula) leaves to the pasta, stirring well. Divide among four warmed pasta bowls. Drizzle with extra virgin olive oil and season to taste. Serves 4

chilli lentils with barbecued veal chops

120 g (4 1/4 oz/2/3 cup) puy lentils or tiny blue-green lentils
1/2 teaspoon sea salt
2 tablespoons olive oil
1 red onion, sliced
1/2 teaspoon garam masala
1 teaspoon ground cumin
1 red chilli, seeded and finely chopped
400 g (14 oz) tin chopped tomatoes
125 ml (4 fl oz/1/2 cup) red wine
1 handful flat-leaf (Italian) parsley, roughly chopped
4 veal chops
green salad, to serve

Put the puy lentils in a saucepan with 500 ml (17 fl oz/2 cups) of water and the salt. Bring to the boil, then reduce the heat and simmer for 30 minutes, or until the lentils are tender. Drain.

Heat the oil in a deep frying pan over medium heat and add the onion, garam masala and cumin. Cook until the onion is soft and the spices are fragrant, then add the chilli, tomato, wine and 125 ml (4 fl oz/1/2 cup) of water. Cook for a further 5 minutes, then stir in the lentils. Simmer over low heat for 10 minutes. Stir in the parsley just prior to serving.

Meanwhile, heat a barbecue chargrill plate, chargrill pan or large frying pan and cook the chops for 2–3 minutes on each side. Remove the chops and serve with the chilli lentils and a green salad. Serves 4

chicken and vegetable pot roast

1.5 kg (3 lb 5 oz) whole organic chicken
1 1/2 tablespoons butter, softened
4 slices of prosciutto
2 onions, cut into eighths
2 large carrots, peeled and cut into chunks
1 celery stalk, cut into 2 cm (3/4 inch) lengths
1 turnip, peeled and cut into chunks
2 leeks, rinsed and cut into 2 cm (3/4 inch) rounds
3 all-purpose potatoes, peeled and cut into chunks
1 rosemary sprig
250 ml (9 fl oz/1 cup) dry white wine
250 ml (9 fl oz/1 cup) chicken stock (Basics)
1 handful flat-leaf (Italian) parsley, roughly chopped

Preheat the oven to 180°C (350°F/Gas 4). Place the chicken in a 3 litre (104 fl oz/12 cup) casserole dish. Rub the butter over the breast of the chicken, then cover with the slices of prosciutto. Arrange the vegetables and rosemary around the chicken, then pour over the wine and stock. Season well with salt and pepper, cover with a lid and bake for 1 hour.

Remove the dish from the oven and gently move the vegetables around. With a large spoon pour some of the juices over the chicken. Return to the oven without the lid and cook for 30 minutes, or until the chicken is golden brown.

Remove the chicken and place it on a serving platter along with the vegetables. Scatter with the parsley and drizzle with the cooking liquid. Serves 4–6

Opposite: chilli lentils with barbecued veal chops
Over: chicken and vegetable pot roast

L. MUIR 1967
19-39

velvet pork belly

800 g (1 lb 12 oz) piece of pork belly
500 ml (17 fl oz/2 cups) chicken stock (Basics)
250 ml (9 fl oz/1 cup) soy sauce
2 red chillies
1 cinnamon stick
4 star anise
1 tablespoon finely grated fresh ginger
2 garlic cloves, crushed
1 1/2 teaspoons Chinese five spice
1 tablespoon grated palm sugar or soft brown sugar
12 fresh shiitake mushrooms
2 tablespoons vegetable oil
100 g (3 1/2 oz) oyster mushrooms, cut in half
100 g (3 1/2 oz) enoki mushrooms, trimmed
steamed greens (Basics), to serve
steamed white rice (Basics), to serve

Preheat the oven to 180°C (350°F/Gas 4). Place the piece of pork belly in a large saucepan and cover with cold water. Bring the water to the boil, then remove the pork and rinse under fresh water.

Put the chicken stock, soy sauce, chillies, cinnamon, star anise, ginger, garlic and 1/2 teaspoon of the five-spice in a 2 litre (70 fl oz/8 cup) casserole dish. Add the pork to the dish, skin side up, and rub the skin with the remaining five-spice. Add enough water to ensure that most of the pork is covered by liquid but the skin is dry. Cover and bake for 4 hours.

Remove the pork from the dish and place onto a large tray. Cover and refrigerate overnight. Strain the liquid, reserving 250 ml (9 fl oz/1 cup).

Pour the reserved cooking liquid into a saucepan and add the sugar, shiitake mushrooms and 125 ml (4 fl oz/1/2 cup) of water and bring to the boil. Reduce the heat to low and allow the sauce to simmer gently for 10 minutes.

Meanwhile, slice the pork belly into 3 x 8 cm (1 1/4 x 3 1/4 inch) strips. Heat the oil in a large non-stick frying pan and fry the strips of pork belly on both sides until they are crisp and browned.

Just prior to serving add the oyster and enoki mushrooms to the saucepan. Place two pieces of pork belly onto each serving plate, then spoon over the mushrooms and sauce. Serve with steamed Chinese greens and white rice. Serves 4

corned beef with white sauce

1.5 kg (3 lb 5 oz) corned beef (silverside)
3 tablespoons soft brown sugar
2 bay leaves
1 star anise
2 cloves
6 peppercorns
2 tablespoons red wine vinegar
2 tablespoons port
8 baby carrots
8 baby onions or 4 onions
4 large pieces of cauliflower

white sauce
2 tablespoons butter
1 onion, finely diced
2 tablespoons plain (all-purpose) flour
500 ml (17 fl oz/2 cups) milk
1 teaspoon salted capers, rinsed and drained
2 tablespoons finely chopped curly parsley
1/4 teaspoon ground white pepper

Put the corned beef in a large saucepan and add the sugar, bay leaves, star anise, cloves, peppercorns, vinegar and port. Fill the pan with water and place over high heat. When the water has come to the boil reduce the heat to low and simmer for 3 hours, skimming the top of any debris and topping up with water to keep the meat fully submerged.

Trim and scrape the carrots. Remove the skin of the onions without removing the top and bottom. If you are using baby onions, leave them intact; if you are using large onions, slice them in half through the stem. About 30 minutes before the beef is cooked, add the vegetables to the pan. Cover and allow the vegetables to slowly cook in the warm liquid.

Meanwhile, to make the white sauce, put the butter and onion in a saucepan and cook over medium heat. When the onion is soft and lightly golden add the flour. Cook for several minutes, stirring often, until the flour turns into a smooth paste that coats the onion. Add the milk a little at a time, working it into the flour, then continue to cook, stirring continuously, for 2–3 minutes until it begins to thicken. Add the capers, parsley and white pepper and stir for a further minute before removing from the heat.

To serve, remove the vegetables from the pan with tongs and divide them among four warmed plates. Remove the beef to a clean cutting board and slice thickly. Divide the slices among the plates and spoon over a little of the cooking liquid and several spoonfuls of white sauce. Serves 4

Opposite: velvet pork belly
Over: corned beef with white sauce

rustic apple and blueberry pie

3 green apples (500 g/1 lb 2 oz in total)
220 g ($7\frac{3}{4}$ oz/1 cup) sugar
grated zest and juice of 1 lemon
250 g (9 oz/2 cups) plain (all-purpose) flour
125 g ($4\frac{1}{2}$ oz) unsalted butter, cut into cubes and chilled
3 tablespoons sugar, extra
2–3 tablespoons chilled water
150 g ($5\frac{1}{2}$ oz/1 cup) blueberries
whipped cream or custard (page 52), to serve

Peel, core and quarter the apples. Place the apple quarters into a saucepan with the sugar, lemon zest, 1 tablespoon of the lemon juice and 750 ml (26 fl oz/ 3 cups) of water. Bring to the boil, then simmer over low heat for 15–20 minutes, or until tender. Remove the apples with a slotted spoon, making sure to drain away as much of the liquid as possible. Cool the apples completely while you continue to simmer the syrup until it has reduced to a third of its original volume, then remove the pan from the heat.

Meanwhile, place the flour in a food processor with the butter and 1 tablespoon of the extra sugar. Process until the mixture begins to resemble breadcrumbs, then add the chilled water. Process briefly until the dough comes together. Remove the dough, cover with plastic wrap and chill in the refrigerator for 10 minutes.

Preheat the oven to 200°C (400°F/Gas 6). Roll the dough out between two large pieces of baking paper into a large circle about 30 cm (12 inches) in diameter. When the dough is uniformly about 5 mm ($\frac{1}{4}$ inches) thick, remove the top sheet of paper and lift the lower sheet of baking paper and dough onto a baking tray. Pile the apples into the centre of the dough, then add the blueberries. Pull the dough up around the sides, scrunching it in over the fruit. Sprinkle with the remaining sugar, then bake for 40 minutes, or until the pastry is golden brown. Remove and allow to cool. Brush some of the apple syrup over the pie before serving. Serve with whipped cream or custard. Serves 6

raspberry pots

300 g ($10\frac{1}{2}$ oz/$1\frac{1}{4}$ cups) frozen raspberries, thawed
3 tablespoons caster (superfine) sugar
$\frac{1}{2}$ teaspoon rosewater
4 large egg yolks
300 ml ($10\frac{1}{2}$ fl oz) pouring (whipping) cream
icing (confectioners') sugar, to serve
fresh raspberries, to serve

Preheat the oven to 140°C (275°F/Gas 1). Purée the raspberries in a blender with the caster sugar, rosewater and egg yolks. Pass through a fine sieve, then stir in the cream.

Sit four ramekins or ovenproof cups in a deep roasting tin and pour the raspberry mixture into them, dividing it evenly. Fill the roasting tin with water until it comes three-quarters of the way up the ramekins. Carefully lift the tin into the oven and bake for 1 hour. The raspberry custard should still be a little soft.

Remove the raspberry pots from the water and allow to cool. Cover with plastic wrap and place in the refrigerator for several hours. Serve chilled with a shake of icing sugar and a tumble of berries. Serves 4

Opposite: rustic apple and blueberry pie
Over: raspberry pots

1000
1
500
1/2

red wine pears

Put 225 g (8 oz/1 cup) caster (superfine) sugar, 350 ml (12 fl oz) red wine, 2 strips of lemon zest, 1 cinnamon stick and 750 ml (26 fl oz/3 cups) of water into a saucepan that is large enough to comfortably fit 6 pears standing upright. Bring the syrup to the boil over high heat, stirring until the sugar has dissolved. Remove from the heat and discard the cinnamon stick. Peel 6 cooking pears, leaving the stems on. Insert the tip of a small sharp knife into the base of the pears and remove the cores with one circular movement. Stand the pears upright in the syrup and cover with a sheet of baking paper. Weigh the paper down with a saucepan lid or saucer, then gently simmer for 1 1/2 hours. To test if the pears are cooked, insert a skewer into the fattest section — they should feel tender. Remove from the heat and allow the pears to cool in the syrup. Serve with sweet mascarpone (page 59). Serves 6

ginger rhubarb

Put 250 g (9 oz/heaped 1 cup) caster (superfine) sugar in a large saucepan with 500 ml (17 fl oz/2 cups) of water. Add 1 star anise and a 4 cm (1 1/2 inch) piece of fresh ginger that has been peeled and cut into thick rounds. Bring to the boil over high heat, stirring to ensure that the sugar dissolves. Reduce the heat to a simmer. Rinse and trim 800 g (1 lb 12 oz/2 bunches) rhubarb, then cut the stalks into 10 cm (4 inch) lengths. Cook the rhubarb in batches in the simmering syrup for 2–4 minutes, or until it begins to soften. Remove the rhubarb with a pair of tongs and place into a deep serving dish. When all the rhubarb has been cooked, increase the heat and reduce the syrup by half. Pour the hot syrup over the rhubarb. Serve warm with custard (page 52) or chilled with vanilla ice cream (Basics) or caramel ice cream. Serves 4–6

vanilla peaches

Rub 2 vanilla beans between your fingertips, then split them in half along their length and put in a large heavy-based saucepan with 220 g (7 3/4 oz/1 cup) sugar and 1 litre (35 fl oz/4 cups) of water. Bring to the boil, stirring until the sugar has dissolved. Reduce the heat to a simmer. Lightly score 6 large peaches along the natural groove. Lower the peaches into the syrup (in batches if necessary) and cover with a piece of crumpled baking paper. Simmer for 5 minutes, rolling the peaches over halfway through cooking if they are not completely covered by the water. Test if the fruit is ready by inserting a skewer into the flesh — it should give but not be too soft. Remove the peaches with a slotted spoon. Bring the syrup to the boil and reduce it by a third. Remove the skin from the fruit, then place the peeled peaches in six bowls. Pour over the syrup. Serve with vanilla ice cream (Basics). Serves 6

slow poached quinces

Put 110 g (3 3/4 oz/1/2 cup) sugar, 2 tablespoons honey, 2 bay leaves and 1 star anise into a saucepan and cover with 500 ml (17 fl oz/2 cups) of water. Stir until the sugar has dissolved. Peel 2 large quinces, then cut into eighths and core the segments. Add the quince segments to the syrup and heat over medium heat until the syrup has come to a slow simmer. Reduce the heat to low, cover with a lid and continue to cook the quinces for 3 1/2 hours, removing the bay leaves after the first hour. When cooked, the quince segments should be soft and the syrup and quinces a wonderful rose colour. Serve the quince segments with a drizzle of syrup and thick (double/heavy) cream or vanilla ice cream (Basics). Serves 4

bake

buttery doughs, crisp crusts,

aromatic roasts and pan juices

Home cooked treats...

There is something deeply comforting about a kitchen filled with the aroma of freshly baked cakes, cookies and breads. It's no longer an everyday occurrence and because of that it feels a little more celebratory. So stoke up the oven, grab that rolling pin, dust the table with flour and bake a little treat that everyone will enjoy.

PIMENTON
222 - by PARKINSON STOVETTE

banana and soy muffins

Preheat the oven to 180°C (350°F/Gas 4). Grease 12 holes of a standard muffin tin or line with paper cases. Mash 2 bananas in a large bowl. Sift 280 g (10 oz/2$\frac{1}{4}$ cups) plain (all-purpose) flour, $\frac{1}{2}$ teaspoon ground cinnamon and 2 teaspoons baking powder over the bananas. Make a well in the centre and add a pinch of salt. In another bowl, whisk together 250 ml (9 fl oz/1 cup) soy milk, 2 eggs, 1 teaspoon natural vanilla extract, 80 g (2$\frac{3}{4}$ oz/$\frac{1}{3}$ cup firmly packed) soft brown sugar and 125 g (4$\frac{1}{2}$ oz) melted butter. Pour the liquid ingredients over the dry and very lightly fold together. Spoon into the prepared muffin holes. Cut a banana into 12 slices and top each muffin with a piece. Combine $\frac{1}{2}$ teaspoon ground cinnamon and 3 tablespoons caster (superfine) sugar and sprinkle over the muffins. Bake for 25 minutes, or until golden and a skewer inserted into the centre comes out clean. Makes 12

cheesy bacon muffins

Preheat the oven to 200°C (400°F/Gas 6). Grease eight holes of a standard muffin tin or line with paper cases. Melt 4 tablespoons butter in a small frying pan over medium heat and cook 3 slices of finely chopped bacon until golden. Remove from the heat. Mix together 200 g (7 oz/heaped 1$\frac{2}{3}$ cups) plain (all-purpose) flour, a pinch of salt, 1 tablespoon caster (superfine) sugar, 2 teaspoons baking powder, 1 handful curly parsley, finely chopped, 2 finely sliced spring onions (scallions) and 2 tablespoons each of grated cheddar and parmesan cheese. Make a well in the centre. Whisk the butter, bacon, 2 eggs and 200 ml (7 fl oz) milk together, add to the dry ingredients and very lightly fold together. Spoon the batter into the muffin holes and sprinkle with a little grated cheddar and parmesan cheese. Bake for 20 minutes, or until golden and a skewer inserted into the centre comes out clean. Serve warm with butter. Makes 8

mixed berry muffins

Preheat the oven to 180°C (350°F/Gas 4). Grease 12 holes of a standard muffin tin or line with paper cases. Put 250 g (9 oz/1 cup) plain yoghurt, 100 ml (3 1/2 fl oz) vegetable oil, 2 eggs and 2 teaspoons natural vanilla extract in a bowl and whisk to combine. Sift 280 g (10 oz/2 1/4 cups) plain (all-purpose) flour and 2 heaped teaspoons baking powder into a large bowl and add 140 g (5 oz/3/4 cup) soft brown sugar and 250 g (9 oz/1 3/4 cups) frozen mixed berries. Stir lightly so that the berries are coated in the flour and are well distributed through the dry ingredients. Add the yoghurt mixture to the dry ingredients and lightly fold together. Spoon into the prepared muffin holes. Top each of the muffins with a large berry and 1 heaped teaspoon raw (demerara) sugar. Bake for 25 minutes, or until the tops are golden and a skewer inserted into the centre comes out clean. Makes 12

carrot and coconut muffins

Preheat the oven to 180°C (350°F/Gas 4). Grease 12 holes of a standard muffin tin or line with paper cases. Sift 280 g (10 oz/2 1/4 cups) plain (all-purpose) flour into a large bowl and add 2 heaped teaspoons baking powder, 200 g (7 oz/scant 1 cup) caster (superfine) sugar, 1/2 teaspoon ground cinnamon, 200 g (7 oz/1 1/4 cups firmly packed) grated carrot and 100 g (3 1/2 oz/heaped 1 cup) desiccated coconut. Stir until combined, then make a well in the centre. In a smaller bowl, beat together 2 eggs, the grated zest and juice of 1 lemon, 1 tablespoon honey and 200 ml (7 fl oz) vegetable oil. Pour the liquid ingredients over the dry and lightly fold together. Spoon the batter into the prepared muffin holes. Bake for 25–30 minutes, or until the muffins are golden brown and a skewer inserted into the centre comes out clean. Serve with a dusting of icing (confectioners') sugar. Makes 12

chocolate and cinnamon breadcrumbs with berries

4 slices of stale sourdough
50 g ($1^{3}/_{4}$ oz/$^{1}/_{2}$ cup) ground almonds
1 tablespoon soft brown sugar
1 tablespoon dark unsweetened cocoa powder
1 teaspoon ground cinnamon
1 tablespoon unsalted butter
250 g (9 oz/$1^{2}/_{3}$ cups) blueberries
250 g (9 oz/2 cups) raspberries
400 g (14 oz) plain or vanilla yoghurt

Preheat the oven to 160°C (315°F/Gas 2–3). Remove the crusts from the bread, then tear the bread into small pieces. Put the bread pieces in a food processor with the ground almonds, sugar, cocoa and cinnamon and process to form fine breadcrumbs. Add the butter and continue blending for a further couple of seconds.

Remove from the food processor and spread out onto a baking tray. Bake in the oven for 10 minutes, or until the crumbs feel crisp. Allow to cool completely. Arrange the berries and yoghurt in a bowl and sprinkle with the chocolate crumbs. Serves 4

orange soda bread with mixed seeds

450 g (1 lb/heaped $3^{2}/_{3}$ cups) plain (all-purpose) flour
1 heaped teaspoon bicarbonate of soda (baking soda)
1 heaped teaspoon cream of tartar
2 tablespoons soft brown sugar
1 tablespoon finely grated orange zest
2 tablespoons sunflower seeds
2 tablespoons poppy seeds
1 tablespoon sesame seeds
1 teaspoon salt
500 ml (17 fl oz/2 cups) buttermilk
2 tablespoons butter, melted
butter, extra, to serve
honey or sliced banana, to serve

Preheat the oven to 200°C (400°F/Gas 6). Sift the flour into a large bowl and add the rest of the dry ingredients and stir to combine. Make a well in the centre and gradually pour in the buttermilk, combining to form a soft dough.

Brush a 10 x 21 cm (4 x $8^{1}/_{4}$ inch) loaf (bar) tin with the melted butter. Scoop the dough into the greased tin and pour over any remaining butter. Bake for 30 minutes, then reduce the oven temperature to 150°C (300°F/Gas 2) and bake for a further 30 minutes, or until a skewer inserted into the centre of the loaf comes out clean.

Turn the bread out onto a wire rack to cool. Serve warm and buttered with honey or sliced banana. Makes 1 loaf

cocoa and berries meet for an indulgent breakfast

Opposite: chocolate and cinnamon breadcrumbs with berries
Over: orange soda bread with mixed seeds

bacon and egg tart

2 1/2 tablespoons butter
3 onions, finely sliced
6 slices of bacon, finely sliced
25 cm (10 inch) prebaked shortcrust tart case (Basics)
4 eggs
2 egg yolks
150 ml (5 fl oz) pouring (whipping) cream
pinch of white pepper
herb salad, to serve

Preheat the oven to 180°C (350°F/Gas 4). Melt the butter in a saucepan over medium heat. Add the onion and cook for 10–15 minutes, or until lightly caramelized. Add the bacon and cook, stirring occasionally, for a further 10 minutes. Spread the bacon and onion over the base of the tart case.

Whisk together the eggs, egg yolks and cream and season with sea salt and white pepper. Pour the mixture carefully into the tart case. Bake for 25 minutes, or until the top of the tart is golden brown. Serve with a herb salad. Serves 6

onion and rosemary focaccia

450 g (1 lb/heaped 3 2/3 cups) plain (all-purpose) flour
1 teaspoon sea salt
15 g (1/2 oz) fresh yeast or 2 teaspoons dried
1 teaspoon sugar
4 tablespoons olive oil
2 tablespoons rosemary
1 small red onion, cut in half and finely sliced
2 tablespoons extra virgin olive oil

Put the (unsifted) flour into a large bowl with the salt. Put the yeast in a small bowl with 310 ml (10 3/4 fl oz/ 1 1/4 cups) of warm water and the sugar. Set aside for 10 minutes. When the mixture has started to froth, add it to the flour along with the oil. Work the ingredients together to form a rough dough before turning it out onto a floured surface. Knead the dough until it is smooth and elastic. Put it into a greased bowl and cover with a tea towel (dish towel). Leave the bowl in a warm place for 1 hour, or until the dough has doubled in size.

Put the dough onto a lightly greased 25 x 37 cm (10 x 14 1/2 inch) baking tray and press it out until it covers the tray. Use your fingers to make dimples in the dough and leave it to rise for a further 20 minutes. Preheat the oven to 200°C (400°F/Gas 6).

Scatter the rosemary over the dough, then top with the sliced onion. Season liberally with sea salt and drizzle with the extra virgin olive oil. Bake the focaccia for 20 minutes, or until the dough is golden brown and cooked through. Cut into small squares and serve warm. Makes 15 squares

sweet onions, salty bacon and creamy eggs

Opposite: bacon and egg tart
Over: onion and rosemary focaccia

baked ricotta with a tomato herb salsa

baked ricotta with a tomato herb salsa

600 g (1 lb 5 oz/heaped 2 1/3 cups) fresh ricotta cheese
1 teaspoon thyme leaves
10 kalamata olives, pitted and roughly chopped
2 tablespoons grated parmesan cheese
1 egg
2 ripe tomatoes
1/2 red onion, finely diced
6 large basil leaves, finely sliced
1 handful flat-leaf (Italian) parsley, roughly chopped
1 teaspoon balsamic vinegar
2 tablespoons extra virgin olive oil
bruschetta (Basics), to serve

Preheat the oven to 180°C (350°F/Gas 4). Cover a baking tray with baking paper.

Put the ricotta in a large bowl with the thyme, olives, parmesan and egg. Stir to combine. Place a 20 cm (8 inch) spring-form cake tin onto a baking tray and spoon the ricotta mixture into the tin. Bake for 35–40 minutes, or until firm and lightly golden. Remove and allow to cool to room temperature.

To make the salsa, slice the tomatoes in half and scoop out the seeds. Finely chop the flesh and place it into a bowl with the onion, basil and parsley. Add the balsamic vinegar and extra virgin olive oil and stir together until well combined.

Transfer the baked ricotta to a serving plate and spoon the salsa over the top. Season with a little salt and a good grind of black pepper. Serve with bruschetta. Serves 6

tomato tarte tatin

1 tablespoon balsamic vinegar
1 tablespoon sugar
1/2 teaspoon thyme leaves
20–24 small truss tomatoes or cherry tomatoes
1 sheet frozen butter puff pastry, trimmed
100 g (3 1/2 oz) buffalo mozzarella cheese
2 tablespoons extra virgin olive oil
green salad, to serve

Preheat the oven to 200°C (400°F/Gas 6). Put the vinegar, sugar and thyme in a non-stick frying pan and place over medium heat. Allow to simmer for a few minutes, stirring until the sugar dissolves, then add the whole tomatoes. Toss the tomatoes in the sweet syrup for a few minutes to ensure they are well coated, then remove from the heat and allow to cool completely in the pan.

Lightly grease the inside edge of a 20 cm (8 inch) pie dish, then arrange the tomatoes over the base and drizzle with the cooking liquid.

Place the sheet of puff pastry over the tomatoes and tuck the edges of the pastry in a little around the tomatoes. Place the pie dish into the preheated oven and bake for 20–25 minutes, or until the pastry is puffed up and golden brown. Place a large serving plate over the top of the pie dish and flip the tart and pan upside down. The tart should now be sitting on the plate with the tomatoes facing up. Tear the buffalo mozzarella into several pieces and scatter over the tart. Drizzle with a little extra virgin olive oil and serve with a green salad. Serves 6

goat's cheese tart

300 g (10 1/2 oz) soft goat's cheese
3 eggs
5 egg yolks
375 ml (13 fl oz/1 1/2 cups) pouring (whipping) cream
25 cm (10 inch) prebaked shortcrust pastry case (Basics)
mixed leaf salad dressed with walnut oil dressing (Basics), to serve

Preheat the oven to 180°C (350°F/Gas 4). In a food processor, blend the goat's cheese, eggs and egg yolks to a smooth purée. Transfer to a bowl, then fold in the cream. Season with sea salt and some freshly ground black pepper.

Place the pre-baked pastry case onto a baking tray, then pour in the cheese filling. Bake for about 30 minutes, or until the top of the tart is lightly golden and the filling is firm. Remove and allow to cool a little.

When the tart is just warm serve with a mixed leaf salad dressed with a walnut oil dressing. Serves 8

hot from the oven: crispy, golden and ready to shar

Opposite: tomato tarte tatin
Over: goat's cheese tart

roast tomato, salami and asparagus orzo

6 roma (plum) tomatoes
12 slices of salami, torn in half
350 g (12 oz/2 bunches) asparagus, trimmed
2 tablespoons olive oil
400 g (14 oz) orzo or risoni
70 g (2 1/2 oz/3/4 cup) shaved parmesan cheese
10 basil leaves, roughly torn
4 tablespoons extra virgin olive oil

Preheat the oven to 180°C (350°F/Gas 4). Line an ovenproof dish with baking paper, ensuring that the paper comes up the sides of the dish.

Cut the tomatoes into quarters, place them into the dish and sprinkle with a little sea salt. Bake the tomatoes for 20 minutes, or until they are quite shrunken. Remove from the oven and cover each wedge of tomato with a piece of salami so that when they cook the oil from the salami will add fabulous flavour to the tomato.

Cut the asparagus spears in half crossways and add them to the dish. Drizzle with the olive oil and return the dish to the oven for 10 minutes.

Bring a large saucepan of salted water to the boil and add the orzo. Cook until *al dente,* then drain and return to the warm pan. Add the tomatoes, salami, asparagus and the juices from the ovenproof dish. Season with a little sea salt and ground black pepper and toss to combine. Pile into a serving dish, add the shaved parmesan and basil leaves and drizzle with the extra virgin olive oil. Serves 4

lemon chicken with parsley salad

2 tablespoons olive oil
4 chicken leg quarters
2 tablespoons dry sherry
3 tablespoons lemon juice
2 tablespoons butter
6 lemon thyme sprigs
4 thin slices of lemon
150 g (5 1/2 oz/1 bunch) flat-leaf (Italian) parsley
250 g (9 oz/2 cups) cherry tomatoes, cut in half
2 tablespoons salted capers, rinsed and drained
1 teaspoon red wine vinegar
3 teaspoons extra virgin olive oil
mashed potato (Basics), to serve (optional)

Preheat the oven to 200°C (400°F/Gas 6). Heat a non-stick frying pan over high heat and add the olive oil. Sear the chicken quarters on both sides until they are golden brown, then transfer to a roasting tin. Season with a little sea salt.

Add 125 ml (4 fl oz/1/2 cup) of water to the roasting tin along with the sherry, lemon juice, butter, thyme sprigs and lemon slices. Bake for 35–40 minutes, or until the chicken is cooked through. To test if the chicken is cooked, insert the point of a sharp knife into the thickest part: the juices should run clear. Cover with foil and allow to rest while you make the salad.

Remove the leaves from the parsley and place into a large bowl with the tomato and capers. Add the vinegar and extra virgin olive oil and toss several times so that the dressing coats the salad. Serve the chicken with the parsley salad in summer or creamy mashed potato in winter. Spoon over the roasting juices. Serves 4

a light flavoursome pasta perfect for summer nights

Opposite: roast tomato, salami and asparagus orzo
Over: lemon chicken with parsley salad

lamb shank and vegetable casserole

80 g (2 3/4 oz/2/3 cup) plain (all-purpose) flour
4 lamb shanks (about 1.25 kg/2 lb 12 oz in total)
160 ml (5 1/4 fl oz) olive oil
2 leeks, rinsed and sliced into rounds
2 garlic cloves, crushed
1 teaspoon rosemary
250 ml (9 fl oz/1 cup) dry sherry
400 g (14 oz) tin chopped tomatoes
2 carrots, peeled and sliced
500 ml (17 fl oz/2 cups) veal stock (Basics)
4 desiree or other all-purpose potatoes, peeled and cut into chunks
gremolata (Basics), to serve

Preheat the oven to 200°C (400°F/Gas 6). Put the flour in a plastic bag, add the shanks and toss until well coated. Heat half the oil in a frying pan and add the lamb shanks. Cook until they are browned on all sides. Transfer the shanks to a casserole dish and wipe the frying pan clean with some paper towels.

Add the remaining oil to the frying pan and cook the leek, garlic and rosemary until the leek is starting to soften. Add the sherry and cook for a few minutes before adding the tomato and carrot. Stir for 1 minute, then pour the sauce over the lamb shanks, add the stock and season with salt and pepper. Cover and bake for 1 hour. Remove from the oven and move the shanks around a little in the sauce. Add the potatoes, cover and return to the oven for a further hour until the meat is tender and falling off the bone. Remove from the oven and serve with a little gremolata. Serves 4

rack of lamb with spinach and white beans

6 ripe roma (plum) tomatoes
500 g (1 lb 2 oz/1 bunch) English spinach, rinsed and trimmed
400 g (14 oz) tin cannellini (white) beans, drained and rinsed
250 ml (9 fl oz/1 cup) veal or beef stock (Basics)
4 anchovy fillets
2 x 8 piece racks of lamb, trimmed

Preheat the oven to 190°C (375°F/Gas 5). Slice the tomatoes in half and place them in a deep roasting tin. Roast the tomatoes for 30 minutes, or until they are beginning to darken and shrivel. Remove the roasting tin from the oven.

Meanwhile, blanch the English spinach in boiling water for a few minutes, then drain and roughly chop.

Add the spinach, beans and stock to the roasting tin. Break the anchovy fillets into small pieces and scatter them over the vegetables.

Heat a large frying pan over high heat and sear the lamb racks on all sides for a few minutes until browned. Place the racks into the roasting tin and return to the oven for 20 minutes. Remove and cover with foil. Allow to rest for 10 minutes. Arrange the vegetables on four warmed plates. Slice the racks into individual cutlets and arrange them over the vegetables. Spoon over some of the roasting juices. Serves 4

Opposite: lamb shank and vegetable casserole
Over: rack of lamb with spinach and white beans

roast beef with wild mushroom butter

2 tablespoons freshly ground black pepper
800 g (1 lb 12 oz) beef eye fillet, trimmed
10 g (1/4 oz) dried porcini mushrooms
2 1/2 tablespoons butter
1 tablespoon dijon mustard
mashed potato (Basics), to serve
steamed asparagus, to serve

Rub the pepper over the beef. Put the beef on a tray and leave it in the refrigerator, uncovered, overnight. Bring to room temperature before cooking.

Preheat the oven to 200°C (400°F/Gas 6). Put the mushrooms in a small bowl, cover with 125 ml (4 fl oz/1/2 cup) of boiling water and soak for 10 minutes, or until soft. Drain, reserving the soaking liquid. Finely chop the mushrooms.

Heat 1 tablespoon of the butter in a small saucepan and add the mushrooms. Cook over medium heat for 5 minutes, then add the soaking liquid. Simmer for 10 minutes, or until most of the liquid has evaporated.

Roughly chop the remaining butter and put it into a bowl. Add the warm mushrooms and mustard and mix well.

Put the fillet into a roasting tin and roast for 10 minutes. Remove the fillet and turn it over before returning to the oven for a further 5 minutes. Remove from the oven, season with sea salt, cover with foil and allow to rest for 15 minutes. Drain any juices from the roasting tin and add them to the mushroom butter. Stir to combine. Return the fillet to the oven for a further 15 minutes. Serve in thick slices topped with some of the mushroom butter, a side dish of creamy mashed potato and steamed asparagus. Serves 4

honey roast chicken with couscous salad

1.8 kg (4 lb) whole organic chicken
35 g (1 1/4 oz/1 bunch) rosemary
1 lemon, cut into quarters
1 onion, cut into quarters
3 tablespoons butter, softened
90 g (3 1/4 oz/1/4 cup) honey
185 g (6 1/2 oz/1 cup) couscous
1 tablespoon finely chopped lime pickle
1 handful flat-leaf (Italian) parsley, roughly chopped
1 handful coriander (cilantro) leaves, roughly chopped
2 tablespoons currants

Preheat the oven to 200°C (400°F/Gas 6). Rinse the chicken and pat it dry with paper towels. Scatter some of the rosemary over the base of a roasting tin, then generously rub the chicken skin with salt and put it on top of the rosemary, breast side up.

Put the lemon, onion and some of the rosemary into the cavity of the chicken, then rub 2 tablespoons of softened butter over the breast. Roast for 1 hour, then drizzle the honey over the chicken. Cook for a further 20 minutes. To check that the chicken is cooked, pull a leg away from the body: the juices that run out should be clear. Rest for 10 minutes before carving.

Place the couscous into a bowl with the remaining butter. Pour over 250 ml (9 fl oz/1 cup) of boiling water, cover the bowl and allow the couscous to stand for 10 minutes. Fluff with a fork and, when cool, stir through the lime pickle, parsley, coriander and currants. Serve the carved chicken with the couscous and a spoonful of the roasting juices. Serves 4

picnic pie

2 tablespoons olive oil
2 onions, grated
750 g (1 lb 10 oz) minced (ground) beef
2 tablespoons tomato paste (concentrated purée)
2 tablespoons soy sauce
2 tablespoons Worcestershire sauce
200 g (7 oz/1 1/3 cups firmly packed) grated carrot
200 g (7 oz/2 cups) grated parsnip
pinch of ground white pepper
2–3 sheets frozen shortcrust pastry
1 egg, beaten
1 tablespoon sesame seeds
good-quality tomato sauce (ketchup), to serve

Preheat the oven to 180°C (350°F/Gas 4). Heat a large frying pan over high heat and add the olive oil and grated onions. Stir until the onion is soft, then add the beef and continue to cook until the meat has browned. Add the tomato paste, soy sauce, Worcestershire sauce, carrot and parsnip. Stir to combine and season to taste with sea salt and ground white pepper. Remove from the heat and allow to cool completely.

Place 1 or 2 pastry sheets into a 26 cm (10 1/2 inch) pie tin, ensuring that the sides are fully covered. Fill the tin with the meat mixture, then cover with the other sheet of pastry. Press the pastry sheets together, rolling the edges over. Brush with the beaten egg and sprinkle with sea salt and sesame seeds. Bake for 30 minutes, or until the pastry is golden. Serve with tomato sauce. Serves 6

Opposite: roast beef with wild mushroom butter
Over: honey roast chicken with couscous salad; picnic pie

spiced currant biscuits

Preheat the oven to 180°C (350°F/Gas 4) and line a baking tray with baking paper. Sift 125 g (4 1/2 oz/1 cup) self-raising flour, 1 1/2 tablespoons ground ginger and 1/2 teaspoon ground cinnamon into a bowl. In another bowl, cream 110 g (3 3/4 oz) softened unsalted butter and 4 tablespoons soft brown sugar until light and fluffy, then beat in 1 egg. Stir in 2 tablespoons maple or dark corn syrup. Fold this mixture through the sifted dry ingredients, then fold in 3 tablespoons currants. Drop teaspoonfuls of the batter onto the tray. Allow some room between each of the biscuits as they will spread a little as they cook. Bake for 12 minutes, or until golden. Cool on a wire rack. To make the lemon glaze, sift 125 g (4 1/2 oz/1 cup) icing (confectioners') sugar into a bowl, then add 1 tablespoon lemon juice. Stir until smooth. When the biscuits are cool, drizzle them with a spiral of lemon glaze. Makes 30

double chocolate treats

Preheat the oven to 180°C (350°F/Gas 4) and line a baking tray with baking paper. Sift 100 g (3 1/2 oz/heaped 3/4 cup) plain (all-purpose) flour and 1 tablespoon unsweetened cocoa powder into a bowl and add 60 g (2 1/4 oz/1/2 cup) each of ground almonds and hazelnuts and a pinch of salt. Cream 125 g (4 1/2 oz) softened unsalted butter and 125 g (4 1/2 oz/heaped 1/2 cup) caster (superfine) sugar together until pale and creamy, then fold in the flour mixture and 1 tablespoon Grand Marnier. Roll teaspoons of the mixture into small balls and place on the tray, then press down to flatten slightly. Bake for 15 minutes until the biscuits look crisp but not too dark. Cool on a wire rack. Melt 100 g (3 1/2 oz) dark eating chocolate and allow to cool. Stir in 100 g (3 1/2 oz/heaped 1/3 cup) sour cream. Sandwich some chocolate cream between two biscuits. Repeat. Dust the biscuits with cocoa and serve. Makes 25

peanut butter cookies

Preheat the oven to 180°C (350°F/Gas 4) and line a baking tray with baking paper. Cream 90 g (3 1/4 oz) softened unsalted butter, 4 heaped tablespoons crunchy peanut butter and 150 g (5 1/2 oz/2/3 cup firmly packed) soft brown sugar until pale, then add 1 egg and stir thoroughly. Sift in 125 g (4 1/2 oz/1 cup) plain (all-purpose) flour, 1/2 teaspoon bicarbonate of soda (baking soda) and 1/4 teaspoon ground cinnamon and mix well. Drop teaspoonfuls onto the tray, leaving room for the cookies to spread. Bake for 12 minutes, then remove the cookies from the oven. Allow them to cool a little on the baking tray before lifting onto a wire rack to cool completely. Makes 35

strawberry swirls

Sift 250 g (9 oz/2 cups) plain (all-purpose) flour and 1/2 teaspoon baking powder into a large bowl, then add 115 g (4 oz/1/2 cup) caster (superfine) sugar. Use your fingertips to rub in 125 g (4 1/2 oz) chopped unsalted butter until the mixture resembles coarse breadcrumbs. Slowly work in 2 lightly beaten eggs until you have a stiff dough. Roll out on a sheet of baking paper into a 20 x 30 cm (8 x 12 inch) rectangle. Spread 100 g (3 1/2 oz/1/3 cup) strawberry jam evenly over the dough and sprinkle with 2 teaspoons ground cinnamon. Roll the dough up, Swiss-roll (jelly-roll) style, from the widest edge, peeling off the paper. Wrap in plastic wrap and refrigerate for 30 minutes. Preheat the oven to 180°C (350°F/Gas 4) and line a baking tray with baking paper. Cut the roll into 1 cm (1/2 inch) slices. Put the rounds on the tray and bake for 15 minutes. Cool on wire racks and dust with icing (confectioners') sugar. Makes 20

peach cake

4 eggs, separated
150 g (5 1/2 oz/1 1/4 cups) plain (all-purpose) flour
1 teaspoon baking powder
150 g (5 1/2 oz/2/3 cup) caster (superfine) sugar
120 g (4 1/4 oz) unsalted butter, melted
1 tablespoon grated lemon zest
2–3 ripe peaches (about 500 g/1 lb 2 oz in total), peeled and cut into thick wedges
icing (confectioners') sugar, to serve

Preheat the oven to 180°C (350°F/Gas 4). Grease and line a 23 cm (9 inch) spring-form cake tin.

Whisk the egg whites until soft peaks form. Sift the flour and baking powder into a bowl, then add the caster sugar. Combine, then make a well in the centre.

In another bowl, whisk together the melted butter, egg yolks and lemon zest. Stir the liquid ingredients and one-third of the egg whites into the well in the dry ingredients until they form a smooth batter, then fold through the remaining egg whites.

Pour into the prepared cake tin. Arrange the peach slices over the top of the cake in a single layer and bake for 30–40 minutes, or until the cake is golden brown and a skewer inserted into the centre comes out clean. Allow to cool, then dust with icing sugar. Serves 8

caramelized apple tartlets

3 small green apples
2 1/2 tablespoons unsalted butter
1 vanilla bean
4 tablespoons caster (superfine) sugar
2 tablespoons brandy
1 sheet ready-made puff pastry
whipped cream, to serve

Preheat the oven to 200°C (400°F/Gas 6). Line a baking tray with baking paper.

Cut the apples into quarters and remove the core. Cut each quarter in half lengthways.

Melt the butter in a frying pan. Rub the vanilla bean between your fingertips to soften it, then split it along its length and use the tip of a knife to scrape out the seeds into the melted butter. When the butter is beginning to bubble, add the apple wedges and cook for 2 minutes on each side. Add the sugar and brandy and cook until the apple starts to caramelize. Remove from the heat.

Cut the puff pastry into four squares and place the squares onto the lined baking tray. Arrange the apples over the pastry and place into the oven. Bake for 20 minutes, or until golden brown. Spoon the remaining syrup over the top and serve with a dollop of whipped cream. Serves 4

summery peaches floating in a lemon-scented cak

Opposite: peach cake
Over: caramelized apple tartlets

passionfruit sponge

2 eggs, separated
115 g (4 oz/1/2 cup) caster (superfine) sugar
70 g (2 1/2 oz/heaped 1/2 cup) plain (all-purpose) flour
1/2 teaspoon baking powder
150 ml (5 fl oz) pouring (whipping) cream, whipped
125 g (4 1/2 oz/1/2 cup) fresh passionfruit pulp
icing (confectioners') sugar, to serve

Preheat the oven to 190°C (375°F/Gas 5). Line the base of a 20 cm (8 inch) round cake tin, then grease it and lightly flour the side and base.

Beat the egg yolks with the caster sugar in a bowl for a few minutes, then add 2 tablespoons of warm water. Continue to beat for a further 8 minutes, or until the mixture is very pale and fluffy.

Sift the flour and baking powder onto a plate. Lightly fold the flour into the egg yolk mixture, a few spoonfuls at a time. In a separate bowl, whisk the egg whites until soft peaks form, then fold the egg whites through the flour mixture. Pour the batter into the tin and bake for 20–25 minutes, or until the sponge springs back when tapped.

Turn out onto a wire rack to cool. When cool, slice in half horizontally. Cover the bottom layer with whipped cream, then spoon over the passionfruit. Place the remaining half on top, then dust with icing sugar. Serves 6

sultana cake

375 g (13 oz/3 cups) sultanas (golden raisins)
250 ml (9 fl oz/1 cup) hot brewed Earl Grey tea
2 tablespoons brandy
350 g (12 oz/scant 1 1/2 cups) caster (superfine) sugar
250 g (9 oz) unsalted butter, softened
3 eggs, lightly beaten
310 g (11 oz/2 1/2 cups) plain (all-purpose) flour
3 1/2 teaspoons baking powder
1/2 teaspoon salt
100 g (3 1/2 oz/2/3 cup) blanched or flaked almonds

Preheat the oven to 180°C (350°F/Gas 4). Grease the base of a 20 cm (8 inch) spring-form cake tin. Line the side of the cake tin with a strip of baking paper that is 1 1/2 times the height of the tin. This will protect the cake as it rises.

Put the sultanas into a bowl and cover with the hot tea and the brandy. Allow to sit for 5 minutes.

Cream the sugar and butter together, then fold in the eggs. Add the hot sultana mixture and stir to combine. Sift in the flour, baking powder and the salt and lightly stir to combine. Spoon the batter into the prepared tin and arrange the almonds over the top. Bake for 1 1/2 hours, or until a skewer inserted into the centre comes out clean. If the cake looks like it is browning too quickly, cover it with a layer of foil. Remove and allow to cool on a wire rack. Serves 10

rhubarb sour cream cake

3 tablespoons unsalted butter, softened
380 g (13 1/2 oz/1 2/3 cups firmly packed) soft brown sugar
2 eggs
1 teaspoon natural vanilla extract
300 g (10 1/2 oz) sour cream
300 g (10 1/2 oz/heaped 2 1/3 cups) plain (all-purpose) flour, sifted
1 teaspoon bicarbonate of soda (baking soda)
1 teaspoon baking powder
400 g (14 oz/1 bunch) rhubarb, roughly chopped
100 g (3 1/2 oz/scant 1/2 cup) caster (superfine) sugar

Preheat the oven to 180°C (350°F/Gas 4). Grease and line a 25 cm (10 inch) spring-form cake tin.

Cream the butter and brown sugar together, then add the eggs, natural vanilla extract and sour cream. Beat well, then sift in the flour, bicarbonate of soda and baking powder and fold together. Spoon the batter into the prepared cake tin. Smooth the top, then lay the rhubarb over the top. Bake for 1 1/2 hours, or until a skewer inserted into the centre comes out clean. If the cake looks like it is browning too quickly, cover it with a layer of foil for the last 30 minutes. Remove and allow to cool on a wire rack. When cool, lift the cake onto a serving plate.

Place the caster sugar in a small saucepan with 100 ml (3 1/2 fl oz) of water. Heat over medium heat until the sugar has melted, then increase the heat to high. Boil the sugar until it is beginning to turn a golden brown, occasionally swirling the pan, but not stirring the mixture. Quickly remove from the heat and spoon the toffee syrup over the rhubarb. Allow to cool before serving. Serves 10

chocolate mousse cake

400 g (14 oz) dark eating chocolate
170 ml (5 1/2 fl oz/2/3 cup) pouring (whipping) cream
3 tablespoons Grand Marnier
6 eggs, separated
1/4 teaspoon ground cinnamon
100 g (3 1/2 oz/1/2 cup) soft brown sugar
unsweetened cocoa powder, to serve
thick (double/heavy) cream or vanilla ice cream (Basics), to serve

Preheat the oven to 150°C (300°F/Gas 2). Grease and line a 23 cm (9 inch) spring-form cake tin.

Put the chocolate and cream into a metal or glass bowl over a saucepan of simmering water, without letting the bowl touch the water. When the chocolate has melted, remove from the heat and stir in the Grand Marnier.

Beat the egg whites until stiff peaks form. In a separate bowl, beat the egg yolks, cinnamon and sugar until thick and fluffy. Fold the chocolate through the egg yolk mixture, then fold the beaten egg whites into the chocolate mixture. Pour the mixture into the prepared tin and bake for 45–50 minutes until a skewer inserted into the cake has some moist, but not wet, mixture on it.

Allow to cool in the tin overnight then, just before serving, turn out onto a serving plate and dust with cocoa. Serve a thin wedge with a dollop of cream or vanilla ice cream. Serves 10

Opposite: sultana cake
Over: rhubarb sour cream cake; chocolate mousse cake

vanilla and almond cake

225 g (8 oz/1 cup) caster (superfine) sugar
200 g (7 oz/1 1/3 cups) blanched almonds
1/2 vanilla bean, finely chopped
250 g (9 oz) unsalted butter, softened and cut into cubes
4 eggs
100 g (3 1/2 oz/heaped 3/4 cup) plain (all-purpose) flour
2 teaspoons baking powder
mixed berries, to serve
icing (confectioners') sugar, to serve
pouring (whipping) cream, to serve

Preheat the oven to 180°C (350°F/Gas 4). Generously grease a 27 cm (10 3/4 inch) bundt or ring tin.

Put the caster sugar and almonds into a food processor with the vanilla bean and process until the vanilla bean has completely broken down and the almonds look like coarse breadcrumbs. Add the butter and continue to process until the mixture is soft and creamy. Add the eggs, flour and baking powder and process until a smooth batter is formed. Spoon the batter into the prepared cake tin.

Bake for 40 minutes, or until a skewer inserted into the centre of the cake comes out clean. If the cake is browning too quickly, cover it loosely with foil. Allow the cake to cool in the tin. Remove the cake when cool and turn out onto a serving plate. Fill the centre with mixed berries and sprinkle with icing sugar. Serve with whipped cream or ice cream. Serves 8–10

lemon tart

23 cm (9 inch) prebaked sweet shortcrust tart case (Basics)
6 lemons
3 eggs
3 egg yolks
175 g (6 oz/3/4 cup) caster (superfine) sugar
250 ml (9 fl oz/1 cup) pouring (whipping) cream
icing (confectioners') sugar, to serve

Preheat the oven to 150°C (300°F/Gas 2) and place the tart case onto a baking tray.

Finely grate the zest of 2 lemons and place it into a large bowl. Juice all of the lemons: you should have around 185 ml (6 fl oz/3/4 cup) of lemon juice. Add it to the lemon zest along with the eggs, egg yolks and caster sugar. Whisk to combine. Add the cream to the lemon mixture and whisk once more before pouring the mixture into the tart case.

Carefully place the tart case into the oven and bake for 35–40 minutes. The lemon filling should be set but will still be a little wobbly in the centre. Remove and allow to cool. Dust with icing sugar before serving. Serves 8

heaven on a plate

Opposite: vanilla and almond cake
Over: lemon tart

basics

savoury recipes

aïoli

2 egg yolks
1 large garlic clove, minced
300 ml ($10^1/_2$ fl oz) light olive oil
juice of 1 lemon
$^1/_4$ teaspoon ground white pepper

Whisk together the egg yolks and garlic with a little sea salt. Slowly start adding the oil in a thin stream, whisking continuously. Add a little of the lemon juice, then continue slowly adding the remaining oil. Gently fold in the remaining lemon juice and season with the white pepper and some sea salt. Makes about 375 ml (13 fl oz/$1^1/_2$ cups)

bruschetta

To make bruschetta, slice the required number of slices from a thick sourdough baguette or country-style loaf. Toast the bread on both sides, then rub a cut garlic clove over the surface. Drizzle with a little olive oil and season with a little sea salt and freshly ground black pepper.

chicken stock

1 whole fresh organic chicken
1 onion, cut into quarters
2 celery stalks, roughly chopped
1 leek, rinsed and roughly chopped
1 bay leaf
a few flat-leaf (Italian) parsley stalks
6 black peppercorns

Rinse the chicken under cold running water and remove any fat from the cavity. Cut the chicken into several large pieces and put them into a large heavy-based saucepan. Cover with 3 litres (104 fl oz/12 cups) of cold water. Bring just to the boil, then reduce the heat to a simmer. Skim any fat from the surface, then add the onion, celery, leek, bay leaf, parsley stalks and peppercorns. Maintain the heat at a low simmer for 2 hours.

Strain the stock into a bowl and allow to cool. Using a large spoon, remove any fat that has risen to the surface. If a concentrated flavour is required, return the strained stock to a saucepan and simmer over low heat. If you are not using the stock immediately, cover and refrigerate or freeze. Makes about 2 litres (70 fl oz/8 cups)

fish stock

1 kg (2 lb 4 oz) fish bones
1 onion, roughly chopped
1 carrot, peeled and roughly chopped
1 fennel bulb, trimmed and sliced
2 celery stalks, roughly chopped
a few thyme sprigs
a few flat-leaf (Italian) parsley stalks
4 black peppercorns

Put the fish bones in a large saucepan with 3 litres (104 fl oz/12 cups) of cold water. Bring just to the boil, then reduce the heat and simmer for 20 minutes. Strain the liquid through a fine sieve into another saucepan to remove the bones, then add the onion, carrot, fennel, celery, thyme, parsley and peppercorns. Return to the boil, then reduce the heat and simmer for a further 35 minutes.

Strain into a bowl and allow to cool. If you are not using the stock immediately, cover and refrigerate or freeze. Makes about 1.5 litres (52 fl oz/6 cups)

gremolata

3 tablespoons finely chopped flat-leaf (Italian) parsley
1 tablespoon finely grated lemon zest
1 tablespoon finely grated fresh horseradish (optional)

Put all the ingredients onto a chopping board and, using a large sharp knife, chop them one more time, working the ingredients together as you chop. Serves 4

mashed potato

1 kg (2 lb 4 oz) all-purpose potatoes
125 ml (4 fl oz/1/2 cup) milk
100 g (3 1/2 oz) butter
pinch of ground white pepper

Peel the potatoes and cut them into chunks. Put the potato into a large saucepan of cold water and bring to the boil. Cook for about 30 minutes. Put the milk and butter into a small saucepan. Warm over a low heat until the butter has melted. When the potato is cooked through, drain and return to the warm pan. Mash while still warm, then whisk in the buttery milk until the potato is soft and creamy. Season with sea salt and white pepper. Serves 4–6 as a side

mashed pumpkin

1 kg (2 lb 4 oz) pumpkin (winter squash)
100 g (3 1/2 oz) butter
1/4 teaspoon ground white pepper
1/4 teaspoon ground cumin
extra virgin olive oil, to serve

Peel the pumpkin and cut it into chunks. Put the pumpkin into a large saucepan of salted cold water and bring to the boil. Boil for 10–12 minutes, or until tender. Drain the pumpkin and return it to the warm pan. Mash while still warm, then whisk in the butter, pepper and cumin. Season to taste with sea salt. Spoon into a warmed serving bowl and drizzle with extra virgin olive oil. Serves 4–6 as a side

pesto

45 basil leaves (2 loosely packed cups)
1 large handful flat-leaf (Italian) parsley, roughly chopped
4 tablespoons roughly grated parmesan cheese
3 tablespoons pine nuts, toasted
1/2 garlic clove
150 ml (5 fl oz) olive oil

To make the pesto, put the basil, parsley, parmesan, pine nuts, garlic and olive oil into a blender or food processor and process until a chunky paste forms. Makes about 250 g (9 oz/1 cup)

polenta

1 teaspoon sea salt
250 g (9 oz/1 2/3 cups) polenta
150 g (5 1/2 oz/1 1/2 cups) grated parmesan cheese
100 g (3 1/2 oz) butter

Bring 1.5 litres (52 fl oz/6 cups) of water to the boil. Add the sea salt, then slowly pour in the polenta while whisking. Reduce the to low heat and cook for 40 minutes at a gentle simmer, stirring from time to time. Add the parmesan and butter and stir until incorporated. Serves 4–6 as a side

roasted capsicums

2–3 capsicums (peppers)
olive oil, for brushing

Preheat the oven to 200°C (400°F/Gas 6). Sit a small rack on or over a baking tray or roasting tin. Lightly rub the capsicums with olive oil and sit them on the rack.

Roast the capsicums for 8–10 minutes, or until the skins begin to blister and blacken — you may need to turn them several times so the skins blister all over.

(If you have a gas stove you can blister the skin by carefully putting the capsicums directly over the flame, turning them around as the skin blisters.) Put the roasted capsicums in a container, cover with plastic wrap and leave to cool — covering them will make them sweat and make them easier to peel.

Remove the blackened skin from the capsicums by gently rubbing it away with your fingertips — it should come away easily. Cut away the stems and seeds from inside the capsicums. The flesh is now ready to eat or use.

shortcrust tart case (savoury)

200 g (7 oz/heaped 1 2/3 cups) plain (all-purpose) flour
100 g (3 1/2 oz) unsalted butter, chilled and cut into cubes
2 tablespoons chilled water

Put the flour, butter and a pinch of salt in a food processor and process for 1 minute. Add the chilled water and process until the mixture comes together. Wrap the dough in plastic wrap and refrigerate for 30 minutes.

Grease a 25 cm (10 inch) tart tin or six 8 cm (3 1/4 inch) tartlet tins. Roll the pastry out as thinly as possible between two layers of plastic wrap, then use the plastic to help you line the prepared tin or tins, removing the plastic wrap once the pastry is in place. Put the tart tin or tins in the refrigerator and chill for a further 30 minutes.

Preheat the oven to 180°C (350°F/Gas 4). Using a fork, prick the pastry case(s) over the base, line with crumpled baking paper and fill with rice or baking weights. Bake for 10–15 minutes, or until the pastry looks cooked and dry. Remove from the oven and allow to cool. Makes 1 large or 6 small cases

Note: The tart case will keep in the freezer for several weeks. There is no need to thaw before using — simply put it in the preheated oven directly from the freezer.

steamed couscous

185 g (6 1/2 oz/1 cup) couscous
1 tablespoon butter

Put the couscous and butter in a large bowl and pour 250 ml (9 fl oz/1 cup) of boiling water over the top. Cover and allow to sit for 5 minutes, then fluff up the grains with a fork. Cover again and leave for a further 5 minutes. Season with a little sea salt and freshly ground black pepper, then rub the grains with your fingertips to remove any lumps. The couscous can be served warm or chilled. Serves 4 as a side dish

steamed greens

500 g (1 lb 2 oz) green vegetables, rinsed and trimmed
extra virgin olive oil or butter, to serve

Bring a large saucepan of water to boil and place a steaming basket over it. Add the greens and steam for 4 –6 minutes. When cooked through, remove the greens and place them into a bowl. Season with sea salt and freshly ground black pepper and toss with a little extra virgin olive oil or butter. Serves 4–6 as a side dish

steamed white rice

200 g (7 oz/1 cup) long-grain white rice

Put the rice in a saucepan with a tight-fitting lid. Cover with 435 ml (15 1/4 fl oz/1 3/4 cups) of water and add a pinch of sea salt. Bring to the boil, then stir once to ensure the grains do not stick to the base of the pan.

Cover the pan and turn the heat down to the lowest setting. Cook the rice for 15 minutes, then take the pan off the heat and allow the rice to sit for a further 10 minutes. Just before serving, fluff up the grains with a fork. Serves 2–4 as a side dish

veal/beef stock

1 kg (2 lb 4 oz) veal or beef bones
2 tablespoons olive oil
2 onions, chopped
3 garlic cloves
2 leeks, rinsed and roughly chopped
2 celery stalks, roughly chopped
2 large tomatoes, roughly chopped
1 bay leaf
6 black peppercorns

Preheat the oven to 200°C (400°F/Gas 6). Put the veal or beef bones and olive oil in a large roasting tin, rub the oil over the bones and roast for 30 minutes. Add the onion, garlic, leek, celery and tomato to the roasting tin. Continue roasting for about 1 hour, or until the bones are well browned.

Transfer the roasted bones and vegetables to a large heavy-based saucepan and cover with 4 litres (140 fl oz/16 cups) of cold water. Bring to the boil over medium heat, then reduce the heat to a simmer. Skim any fat from the surface, then add the bay leaf and peppercorns. Cook at a low simmer for 4 hours.

Strain the stock into a bowl and allow to cool. Using a large spoon, remove any fat from the surface. Return the stock to a clean saucepan and simmer over low heat to reduce and concentrate the flavour. If you are not using the stock immediately, cover and refrigerate or freeze. Makes about 2 litres (70 fl oz/8 cups)

vegetable stock

2 tablespoons unsalted butter
2 garlic cloves, crushed
2 onions, roughly chopped
4 leeks, rinsed and roughly chopped
3 carrots, peeled and roughly chopped
3 celery stalks, thickly sliced
1 fennel bulb, trimmed and roughly chopped
1 handful flat-leaf (Italian) parsley
2 thyme sprigs
2 black peppercorns

Put the butter, garlic and onion in a large heavy-based saucepan. Put the pan over medium heat and stir until the onion is soft and transparent. Add the leek, carrot, celery, fennel, parsley, thyme and peppercorns. Add 4 litres (140 fl oz/16 cups) of cold water and bring to the boil. Reduce the heat and simmer for 2 hours. Allow the stock to cool.

Strain the stock into a clean saucepan, using the back of a large spoon to press the liquid from the vegetables. Bring the stock to the boil, then reduce the heat to a rolling boil until the stock is reduced by half. If you are not using the stock immediately, cover and refrigerate or freeze. Makes about 2 litres (70 fl oz/8 cups)

walnut oil dressing

1 tablespoon walnut oil
2 tablespoons olive oil
1 tablespoon red wine vinegar
1/2 teaspoon honey

Whisk the ingredients together and season with a little sea salt and freshly ground black pepper. Makes about 80 ml (2 1/2 fl oz/1/3 cup)

sweet recipes

almond biscotti

125 g (4 1/2 oz/1 cup) plain (all purpose) flour
115 g (4 oz/1/2 cup) caster (superfine) sugar
1 teaspoon baking powder
150 g (5 1/2 oz/1 2/3 cups) flaked almonds
1 teaspoon grated lemon zest
1/4 teaspoon ground cinnamon
2 eggs, beaten

Preheat the oven to 180°C (350°F/Gas 4) and line a baking tray with baking paper. Sift the flour into a large bowl and add the rest of the dry ingredients. Make a well in the centre and fold in the eggs to make a sticky dough. Turn it out onto a clean floured surface.

Divide the dough into two portions and roll out each portion to form a log approximately 4 cm (1 1/2 inches) wide. Put the logs onto the tray, leaving space between each log to spread a little. Bake for 30 minutes. Remove and allow to cool. Reduce the oven temperature to 140°C (275°F/Gas 1). With a sharp bread knife, cut each of the logs into thin slices approximately 5 mm (1/4 inch) wide. Lay the slices on a baking tray and return them to the oven. Bake for 20–25 minutes, turning the biscuits once. Remove from the oven and cool on wire racks. Makes 30–40

meringues

2 egg whites
100 g (3 1/2 oz/scant 1/2 cup) caster (superfine) sugar

Preheat the oven to 120°C (235°F/Gas 1/2). Line a baking tray with baking paper. Beat the egg whites until soft peaks form, then gradually add half the sugar, beating the mixture quite fast for 2 minutes until stiff peaks form. Remove the beaters and lightly fold through the remaining sugar. Spoon the mixture into large dollops on the baking tray, then bake for 1 1/2 hours. Turn the oven off, leaving the door open and allow the meringues to cool in the oven. Store in an airtight container until ready to use. Makes 8

scones

400 g (14 oz/3 1/4 cups) plain (all-purpose) flour
3 teaspoons baking powder
2 tablespoons caster (superfine) sugar
85 g (3 oz) unsalted butter, chilled and diced
1 teaspoon lemon juice
200 ml (7 fl oz) milk
2 eggs

Preheat the oven to 200°C (400°F/Gas 6). Line a baking tray with baking paper. Sift the flour into a large bowl. Add the baking powder, sugar, butter and a pinch of salt. Rub the butter into the flour until it resembles fine breadcrumbs. In a separate bowl, stir the lemon juice into the milk, then whisk in the eggs. Make a well in the centre of the dry ingredients and pour in the milk mixture. Stir until the ingredients just come together, then turn out onto a floured surface. Knead once or twice to just bring the dough together.

Press the dough out until it is 3–4 cm (1 1/4–1 1/2 inches) thick. Using a round cookie cutter, cut out rounds of dough and put them onto the tray. Bake for 12 minutes, or until golden. Makes 15

shortcrust tart case (sweet)

200 g (7 oz/heaped 1 2/3 cups) plain (all-purpose) flour
100 g (3 1/2 oz) unsalted butter, chilled and cut into cubes
1 tablespoon caster (superfine) sugar
2 tablespoons chilled water

Put the flour, butter, sugar and a pinch of salt in a food processor and process for 1 minute. Add the chilled water and process until the mixture comes together. Wrap the dough in plastic wrap and refrigerate for 30 minutes.

Grease a 25 cm (10 inch) tart tin or six 8 cm (3 1/4 inch) tartlet tins. Roll the pastry out as thinly as possible between two layers of plastic wrap, then use it to line the prepared tin or tins, removing the plastic wrap once the pastry is in place. Chill for a further 30 minutes.

Preheat the oven to 180°C (350°F/Gas 4). Using a fork, prick the pastry case(s) over the base, line with crumpled baking paper and fill with rice or baking weights. Bake for 10–15 minutes, or until the pastry looks cooked and dry. Remove from the oven and allow to cool. Makes 1 large or 6 small cases

Note: The tart case will keep in the freezer for several weeks. There is no need to thaw before using – simply put it in the preheated oven directly from the freezer.

sterilizing jars

First check that the jars have no cracks or chips. Wash well in hot soapy water, rinse thoroughly in very hot water and place in an oven preheated to 150°C (300°F/Gas 2) for 30 minutes. If you are using jars with screw-top lids, submerge the clean lids in boiling water for 10 minutes. Remove and allow to dry in the oven.

vanilla ice cream

375 ml (13 fl oz/1 1/2 cups) milk
250 ml (9 fl oz/1 cup) pouring (whipping) cream
2 vanilla beans
4 egg yolks
150 g (5 1/2 oz/2/3 cup) caster (superfine) sugar

Pour the milk and cream into a heavy-based saucepan. Lightly rub the vanilla beans between your fingertips to soften them. Split the beans in half along their length and put them in the pan. Put the saucepan over medium heat and bring the mixture just to simmering point. Remove the pan from the heat.

Whisk the egg yolks with the caster sugar in a large bowl until light and creamy. Whisk in a little of the warm milk mixture before adding the remaining liquid. Remove the vanilla beans and whisk to combine.

Rinse and dry the saucepan, then return the mixture to the clean pan. Scrape the inside of the vanilla beans to remove the last of the seeds, then add these to the mixture. Cook over medium heat, stirring constantly with a wooden spoon, until the mixture thickens and coats the back of the spoon. Remove quickly and strain into a chilled bowl. Allow to cool completely before churning in an ice-cream machine according to the manufacturer's instructions. Spoon into a container and freeze for at least 1 hour until ready to serve.

If you don't have an ice-cream machine, you can make it in your freezer though the texture will suffer a little. Pour the ice cream base into a metal bowl. Cover with plastic wrap and freeze. Every hour stir the ice cream with a fork, scraping the frozen base from the side and folding it back through the ice cream. Repeat until the ice cream is quite stiff and then freeze overnight. Makes 1 litre (35 fl oz/4 cups)

glossary

american-style pork ribs
These are pork ribs that are trimmed from the inside of the belly and they still have quite a bit of meat attached. They generally come as a rack but often butchers will trim them into pairs.

anchovy fillets
A small fish normally sold filleted and cured in either salt or olive oil. They can be bought tinned from supermarkets or preserved in oil from most delicatessens and speciality food stores.

balsamic vinegar
Balsamic vinegar is a dark, aged vinegar made from grape juice. It is valued for its fragrant, sweetish taste. Bottles of authentic balsamic vinegar are labelled 'Aceto Balsamico Tradizionale de Modena'.

bocconcini cheese
These are small balls of fresh mozzarella, often sold sitting in their own whey. When fresh, they are soft and springy to the touch and have a milky taste. Cherry bocconcini are smaller bite-sized versions. Both are available from delicatessens and some supermarkets.

brioche
Brioche is a light, sweet French-style bread which is flavoured with eggs and butter. Its rich colouring and fine texture make it ideal for breakfast dishes and for desserts. It can be bought from bakeries and some large supermarkets.

broad beans
Broad beans or fava beans can be eaten whole when they are very young but are more commonly sold as large, flat beans which need to be shelled like peas. The resultant beans are then cooked and peeled of the outer tough skin to reveal delicate bright green beans. When fresh beans are not in season the shelled bean can be bought frozen in most large supermarkets.

broccolini
Broccolini is a cross between gai larn and broccoli, resulting in a green vegetable with long, thin stems and small florets. It is ideal for steaming, blanching and stir-frying.

buttermilk
This cultured, low-fat dairy product is made from skim milk and milk powder and has a tart taste. It is often used in baking as a raising agent and can be found in cartons in the refrigerated section of most supermarkets.

cannellini beans
These are small white beans most commonly used in soups and salads. They can be bought dried or pre-cooked in tins.

capers
Capers are the green buds from a Mediterranean shrub, preserved in brine or salt. Salted capers have a firmer texture and better flavour and are often smaller than those preserved in brine.

cardamom
A dried seed pod native to India. When crushed, the seeds give off a sweet, strong aroma. It is used whole or ground. Use sparingly, as it has a strong flavour.

casareccia
These short lengths of rolled and twisted Italian pasta are traditionally served with a meat sauce.

chinese five-spice
An aromatic mix of ground spices, Chinese five-spice is made from star anise, black pepper, fennel seeds, cassia and cloves.

chinese roasted duck
Whole ducks that have been rubbed with Chinese spices, then roasted until the skin is crispy and a glossy golden brown. They can be bought freshly cooked in speciality Chinese stores and butchers.

ciabatta bread
An Italian style bread which is sold in long, flattish loaves. It is flavoured with olive oil and has a crisp crust.

cinnamon
Commonly sold in powdered form, cinnamon can also be bought in long 'quills' of bark, sometimes up to 1 metre (3 feet) long.

couscous
The favoured dish of North Africa, couscous is made from a flour-coated granular semolina, which is traditionally steamed in a *couscousiere*. Today, instant couscous is available in most large supermarkets.

crème fraîche
A naturally soured cream that is lighter than sour cream, crème fraîche is available at gourmet food stores and some large supermarkets. Sour cream can usually be used as a substitute.

cumin
Cumin can be obtained in a pre-ground powder but its flavour is more pronounced when it is dry-roasted in a pan or oven and then freshly ground in a spice grinder.

dried mushrooms
Dried mushrooms are available in most speciality food stores. Soak in hot water before use.

enoki mushrooms
These pale, delicate mushrooms have long, thin stalks and tiny caps. They are very fragile and need only minimal cooking. They are bland in flavour but have an interesting texture and appearance so are ideal for blending with other mushrooms.

fennel
A white, large-bulbed vegetable with a feathery green top, fennel can be eaten raw in salads or baked. It has a soft aniseed flavour. The seeds are used as a spice.

fish sauce
This pungent, salty liquid made from fermented fish is widely used in Southeast Asian cooking to add a salty, savoury flavour.

french or red asian shallots
These small onions have a thin, papery skin and grow in bunches. Sometimes called eschallots or échalotes.

garam masala
An Indian spice blend that features ground coriander, cumin, cardamom, cloves and nutmeg.

gelatine leaves
Leaf gelatine is available in sheets of varying sizes. Be careful to check the manufacturer's instructions regarding the ratio of liquid to gelatine. If leaves are unavailable, use gelatine powder instead.

goat's cheese
This is a soft, fresh cheese made from goat's milk. It has a slightly acidic but mild and creamy flavour.

golden syrup
A light golden coloured syrup that has a thick consistency similar to honey. It is used to flavour puddings and other sweet recipes.

jerusalem artichokes
No relation to the globe artichoke, these small tubers are in fact a cousin of the sunflower. Their sweet earthy flavour makes them ideal for using in soups and purées.

lemon grass
These long, fragrant stems are very popular in Thai cuisine. The tough outer layers should be stripped off first, then the white inner part of the stem can be used either finely chopped or whole to flavour soups and broths.

lime pickle
A spiced Indian-style pickle made with limes. It can be bought in Indian speciality stores or most large supermarkets.

maple syrup
A rich brown syrup obtained from the sap of certain Canadian and American maple trees.

marsala
A fortified wine from Italy, which in its dry form is traditionally used to flavour veal dishes, while the sweet version is used to enrich the flavour of many cream-based desserts.

mascarpone
This heavy, Italian-style set cream is used as a base in many sweet and savoury dishes. It is made from cream so is high in fat. It is sold in delicatessens and supermarkets.

mirin
Mirin is a rice wine used in Japanese cooking. It adds sweetness to sauces and dressings, and is used for marinating and glazing dishes. It is available from Asian grocery stores and most supermarkets.

mozzarella cheese
Fresh mozzarella can be found in most delicatessens and is identified by its smooth, white appearance and ball-like shape. It is not to be confused with mass-produced mozzarella, which is mostly used as a pizza topping. Mozzarella is usually sold packed in whey. Buffalo mozzarella is considered the best.

mustard seeds
Mustard seeds have a sharp, hot flavour that is tempered by cooking. Both brown and yellow seeds are available, although brown mustard seeds are more common.

natural vanilla extract
When using vanilla extract, ensure it is made from real vanilla and is not labelled 'imitation' vanilla extract or essence. The flavours are quite different, with the imitation being almost acrid in its aftertaste. *See also* vanilla bean.

orzo
Small rice-shaped pasta often used in soups.

oyster mushrooms
These beautifully shaped, delicately flavoured mushrooms are commonly white or a pale, greyish brown, but can also be pink or yellow. They are also called abalone mushrooms. Their flavour is quite sharp when raw, making them suitable for creamy pasta or stir-fried dishes.

palm sugar
Palm sugar is obtained from the sap of various palm trees and is sold in hard cakes or cylinders and in plastic jars. If it is very hard it will need to be grated. It can be found in Asian grocery stores and large supermarkets. Soft brown sugar can be used instead.

pancetta
This is salted belly of pork and it is somewhat like streaky bacon. It can be bought either rolled and finely sliced or in large pieces. It is available from delicatessens and some supermarkets.

panettone
An aromatic northern Italian bread made with raisins and candied peel. Panettone is traditionally eaten at Christmas, when it is found in Italian delicatessens or large supermarkets.

papaya
This large tropical fruit can be red, orange or yellow. It contains an enzyme that stops gelatine setting, so avoid using it in jellies. It is sometimes called a pawpaw, but this is really part of the custard apple family

pecorino cheese
Strong flavoured, hard cheese made from sheep's milk. It is quite similar to parmesan cheese in flavour.

polenta
A yellow grainy cornmeal, which is slowly cooked in boiling water to form a thick, savoury porridge.

pomegranate
Large red fruit which features in Middle Eastern cooking. Only the small jewel-like seeds are eaten – they provide a tart sweetness.

pomegranate molasses
This is a thick syrup made from a reduction of pomegranate juice. It has a bitter-sweet flavour. It is available from Middle Eastern speciality stores. The closest substitute is sweetened tamarind.

pork belly
A cut of meat taken from the underside of a pig. This particular section is commonly used for

streaky bacon and pancetta but pieces can also be slow-cooked, providing a rich and succulent meat.

preserved lemon
These are whole lemons preserved in salt or brine, making their rind soft and pliable. Only the rind is used – the bitter, salty pulp should be scraped out and thrown away. Preserved lemons are available from many delicatessens.

prosciutto
Prosciutto is lightly salted, air-dried ham. It is most commonly sold in paper-thin slices at delicatessens. Parma ham and San Daniele are both types of prosciutto.

puy lentils
Originally grown in the volcanic soils of the Puy region in France, these lentils are highly prized for their flavour and the fact that they hold their shape during cooking.

radicchio
A member of the chicory family, this Italian-style green has bitter flavoured red leaves.

ricotta cheese
Ricotta cheese can be bought cut from a wheel or in tubs, in normal and low-fat versions. The wheel tends to be firmer in consistency and is better for baking as is the ricotta with the higher fat content. If you are only able to purchase the tub ricotta, drain off excess moisture by letting it sit for 2–3 hours in a sieve lined with muslin (cheesecloth).

risoni
Risoni are small rice-shaped pasta ideal for use in soups or salads.

risotto rice
There are three well known varieties of risotto rice widely available. Arborio, a large plump grain that makes a sticky risotto; vialone nano, a shorter grain that produces a loose consistency and maintains more of a bite in the middle; and carnaroli, of a similar size to vialone nano, which makes a risotto with a good, firm consistency. All varieties or risotto rice are interchangeable, although cooking times may vary by 5 minutes.

rosewater
The distilled essence of rose petals, rosewater is used in small quantities to impart a perfumed flavour to pastries, fruit salads and puddings.

sea salt
Sea salt is a type of table and cooking salt obtained through a process of natural evaporation. It is a little more expensive than regular salt, but its superior flavour easily justifies the extra cost. It is sold in a range of grades, from fine grains through to flakes and coarse granules.

sesame oil
Sesame oil is available in two varieties. The darker, more pungent type is made from roasted sesame seeds and comes from China, while the paler, non-roasted variety is Middle Eastern in origin.

sesame seeds
These tiny seeds, which grow in pods on several varieties of sesame plant, are reputed to be the world's oldest seasoning. White seeds are the most common, but there are also black, brown and red varieties. To enhance the flavour, lightly toast sesame seeds before using.

shiitake mushrooms
These Asian mushrooms have white gills and a brown cap. Meaty in texture, they keep their shape well when cooked. Dried shiitake are often sold as dried Chinese mushrooms.

smoked paprika
Paprika is commonly sold as a dried, rich red powder made from a member of the chilli family. It is sold in many grades, from delicate through to sweet and hot. Smoked paprika from Spain adds a distinct rich, smoky flavour.

sourdough
Sourdough is a French-style bread which uses a fermented dough as its raising agent. It is commonly a thick-textured country-style loaf.

star anise
This is a pretty, star-shaped dried fruit containing small oval, brown seeds. It has a flavour similar to anise, but is more liquorice-like.

sumac
Sumac is a peppery, sour spice made from dried and ground sumac berries. The fruit of a shrub found in the northern hemisphere, it is typically used in Middle Eastern cookery. Sumac is available from most large supermarkets and Middle Eastern speciality stores.

tahini
This is a thick, creamy paste made from ground white sesame seeds. It is used to give a strong nutty flavour to Middle Eastern salads or sauces. Tahini is sold in jars in health-food stores and most supermarkets.

truss tomatoes
Truss tomatoes are simply those that are sold still on the vine.

turmeric
Though occasionally available fresh, turmeric is more commonly seen in its dried and ground form as a spice.

vanilla bean
This long, slim, black bean has a wonderful caramel aroma that synthetic vanilla can never capture. Good-quality beans are soft and not too dry.

walnut oil
A richly flavoured oil it is perfect for use in dressing salads that accompany cheese, pear or shellfish.

white pepper
White pepper is produced by removing the outer husk of the black peppercorn. It has a little more 'bite' than black pepper, yet without the overriding flavour. It is more commonly used in white sauces on account of its colour, but it is also wonderful in rich or creamy dishes that you wish to balance with a little heat.

wild rocket
A smaller version of the large-leafed rocket (arugula), wild rocket has delicate leaves but a strong peppery flavour that is perfect in salads.

yeast
Yeast is used as a raising agent for specific bread doughs. It is available dried in sachets from supermarkets or fresh from speciality food stores.

index

This edition first published in Canada in 2006 by Whitecap Books, 351 Lynn Ave., North Vancouver, British Columbia, Canada, V7J 2C4.
www.whitecap.ca

First published by Murdoch Books Pty Limited in 2006.
www.murdochbooks.com.au

Chief executive: Juliet Rogers
Publisher: Kay Scarlett

Design concept and design: Marylouise Brammer
Design manager: Vivien Valk
Project manager: Jacqueline Blanchard
Editor: Zoë Harpham
Photographer: Mikkel Vang
Stylist: Christine Rudolph
Food preparation: Ross Dobson
Recipe testing: Michelle Lucia
Production: Adele Troeger
Photographer's assistant: Andrew Wilson
Stylist's assistant: Britt Vinther-Jensen

ISBN 1-55285-827-8
ISBN 978-1-55285-827-1

Printed by 1010 Printing International Limited in 2006. PRINTED IN CHINA. First published 2006.

IMPORTANT: Those who might be at risk from the effects of salmonella poisoning (the elderly, pregnant women, young children and those suffering from immune deficiency diseases) should consult their doctor with any concerns about eating raw eggs.

CONVERSION GUIDE: You may find cooking times vary depending on the oven you are using. For fan-forced ovens, as a general rule, set the oven temperature to 20°C (35°F) lower than indicated in the recipe. We have used 20 ml (4 teaspoon) tablespoon measures. If you are using a 15 ml (3 teaspoon) tablespoon, for most recipes the difference will not be noticeable. However, for recipes using baking powder, gelatine, bicarbonate of soda (baking soda) or small amounts of cornflour (cornstarch), add an extra teaspoon for each tablespoon specified.

The Publisher and stylist would like to thank Le Creuset, Joan Platt Ceramics NYC, Womkiware, Kris Coad, Allan Fox, Step Back antiques, Calvin Klein homewares, Manon, Granny's Market, Bennington ceramics, MUD Australia, Object Paradiso, Claire Coles UK, Christiane Perrochon Italy, Scullerymade, Est Est Est, Dean & Delucca NYC, Indeco Wood Tasmania, Empire 111 for lending equipment for use and photography. Also a huge thank you to Bringalbit Country Retreat (www.bringalbit.com.au) for allowing us to photograph on location.